We Wove a Web in Childhood

An extraordinary drama about the Brontës.

Cally Phillips

First published by HoAmPresst Publishing in 2013

This new edition is published in 2016 to commemorate the start of the Brontë Bicentenary

HoAmPresst Publishing
An imprint of
Ayton Publishing Limited
Hillhead of Ardmiddle
Turriff,
Aberdeenshire AB53 8AL

Contact aytonpublishing@gmail.com

ISBN 978-1-910601-31-0

Cover images are from the original production.

For Kate and Emily.

'Heathcliff, it's me, your Cathy, I've come home…'

'…Nelly, I am Heathcliff.'

This play was first performed from August 30th to September 18th 1993 at the Duke's Head Theatre, Richmond.

Original cast:

Charlotte Brontë: Valeria Fabbri.

(In Angria, Charlotte is Arthur Wellesley the Marquis of Douro and Duke of Zamorna. Also Northangerland's mother)

Branwell Brontë: Thomas Anderson.

(In Angria, Branwell is Alexander 'Rogue' Percy, the Duke of Ellrington and Earl of Northangerland. Also Howard Warner. In Gondal, Branwell is King Julius Brenazaida)

Emily Brontë: Annette Bullen

(In Angria, Emily is Lady Zenobia Ellrington. Also Mary Percy. In Gondal, Emily is Queen Augusta.)

Anne Brontë: Anna Soderblom

(In Angria Anne is Montmorency. Also Edward Sydney and Louisa Vernon)

Each Brontë also takes on the role of various 'minor' characters throughout the play.

CONTENTS:

Introduction

Staging

THE PLAY

Act 1 Scene 1: 1848: Brontë Parsonage.

Act 1 Scene 2: 1826: Brontë Parsonage

Act 2 Scene 1: 1832: Angria, Battlefield.

Act 2 Scene 2: Verdopolis (The Angrian Capital)

Act 2, Scene 3: Verdopolis – Major Selby's Ball

Act 2, Scene 4: Verdopolis – Ellrington's Hall

Act 2, Scene 5: 1836: Angria, Battlefield

Act 2, Scene 6: Angria – Zamorna's Mansion

Act 2, Scene 7: 1838: Angria, Northangerland's House/ Battlefield .

Act 3,Scene 1: 1838: Angria.

Act 3, Scene 2: Angria

Act 3, Scene 3: 1840: Angria.

Act 3, Scene 4: 1840: Brontë Parsonage,

Act 3, Scene 5: 1839/1841/1845 Brontë Parsonage.

Act 3, Scene 6: 1845: Brontë Parsonage/ Gondal.

Act 3, Scene 7: Gondal

Act 3, Scene 8: Gondal

Act 3, Scene 9: 1848: Brontë Parsonage.

About Cally Phillips – A Life in Stages.

INTRODUCTION

Kate Bush led me to the Brontës. I can still remember the first time I heard 'Wuthering Heights' on the radio. I stood in the kitchen as it came on the radio marvelling at its unique weirdness. I was seventeen. I found it so compellingly strange that I just had to read the novel to see if I could make sense of the song. I have been trying to make sense of both ever since. Both have remained strong creative influences. Indeed it is thanks to Kate and Emily that I am the writer (and woman) I am today.

Given this, it is perhaps not surprise that my first adult attempt to write should involve the Brontës. At seventeen I tried, and failed to write plays, prose and pop songs. All my 'juvenilia' found its worth in the bin. But it was the start of a lifelong attempt to do justice on paper to the thoughts in my head. It was roughly a decade later that I gained the confidence to try again. In 1989-90, I embarked upon my first stageplay: *'We Wove a Web in Childhood'*. Looking back with the benefit of more than twenty five years hindsight, I realise that the task I took on was less that of playwright and more that of editor or dramaturge. I felt my way into creativity vicariously using the Brontës as my guide Through the best part of a year of research I read all that I could of the Brontë juvenilia, many of them poor copies of the tiny handwriting, and I

7

turned them into a speculative chronological story. In the process I felt I was discovering something important about the relationships and tensions of the growing siblings.

The story of the Brontës is well known. Perhaps at times it is too well known, in that the 'knowledge' has taken over from the facts, leaving little room for speculation, which I contend is all that we really have to go on when dealing with the past. Our relationship with the past is always refracted through the prism of our beliefs. Imagination is key to the process, in my opinion.

In the case of the Brontës, their first 'juvenile' writings date from 1826 when Charlotte was ten. The three sisters and one brother kept on writing until their respective deaths. My intention in *'We Wove A Web in Childhood'* was to let the Brontës speak out, but also to take a speculative contextualisation of their writing as reflective of their actual lived experiences.

The play was completed in 1990, and I spent the next two years trying to get interest for a staged production. Everywhere I went the answer was the same. Interesting, but impossible to stage. I knew this was wrong. I could see exactly how it might be staged. So in 1993 I took the plunge and directed it myself. We had a two week run at a London fringe venue. The stage was a 12ft square 'black box' above a pub and in that space we created the sort of magic that only live theatre can.

Ephemeral magic, but it proved to me (and others) that the play was indeed, stage-able. Unless you were there of course, you have to take my word for it.

Audience reactions (including reservations) were interesting. Most people bought into the fantasy, but I remember one earnest woman coming up to me after a performance, telling me how much she had enjoyed it but (heavy emphasis) she was adamant that I should realise that of course it couldn't have been like that. They were well brought up young women. They would not have acted out their stories. I disagreed then and I disagree now. The notion of the Bronte sisters as prim, proper and aloof has taken (reasonably) quite a battering in recent years as we have looked more closely into their lives and times. We like to revere creative genius, but it is important to also bear in mind that children are children – and they like to play. They are imaginative. Children acting out their fantasies is not unusual. Writing them down is. But the writing was, in my opinion, just part of the play.

For me at least, drama is both the province of the imagination and offers the ultimate counterfactual. It's a world in which a girl *can* become the Duke of Wellington and the Battle of Waterloo *can* be played out to the death with four participants in the sitting room, before tea time. And what better way to make your sibling suffer than impose psychological distress on their very deepest sense

9

of identity? In writing the play I played with a range of 'what ifs?' For example: 'What if Charlotte and Branwell were so angry with each other that they chose to kill of the other's character as a way of expressing their anger?' Once I started asking 'why did she write it that way?' 'Why did they make that choice?' I found I was half way towards something quite extraordinary.

I believe that this play is still the only theatrical attempt to draw some kind of chronological 'perspective' on how the created stories parallel the lives and actual relationships between the Brontës . It might be too easy to see the Brontës themselves as 'characters' in this play but the real interest is in the interplay between reality and fiction in their lives. I believe that the 'storied' nature of the Brontë's writings may offer an important insight into their lives. They used characters in many creative ways - and the blurring between fiction and fact which is laid out in this play is a kind of speculation.

The Brontës gave the inspiration and the text. What I brought to the party was the suggestion that the juvenile narratives also contain some insight into the relationships between the siblings. This is now a much more accepted view than I found it in the early 1990s. I do not claim to have 'got it right' or to represent them accurately – but I hope the play makes the audience (or reader) consider the possibilities offered by the text and staging.

Brontë juvenilia is much more accessible now than when I wrote and produced this play. Thus individuals can explore possibilities for themselves and come up with their own conclusions. For anyone interested in the Brontës the first ports of call are the writings of Christine Alexander and Juliet Barker, and I would direct anyone interested either in the Brontës or this play, to their work.

I still hold my head up high over my first play: '*We Wove a Web in Childhood*' after all this time. I still believe it offers a possible 'reading' of the work and lives of the Brontës which is both interesting and significant. And I still contend that it offers a remarkable opportunity for female actors to explore a range of character rarely afforded on the stage. For all these reasons I hope that during the Bronte bicentennial years it will be taken out of the 'treasure chest' once more, dusted down and performed with new actors, new direction and new vigour. It is stage-able. I hope the time may be ripe for a reappraisal of the significance of their juvenilia and the worlds of Angria and Gondal, as well as a reappraisal of the possible insights their work gives us into their lives. It's all speculation, but what fun we can have imagining.

Cally Phillips.

While one could of course play this on a traditional proscenium arch stage, and of course any new production should explore its own ways, we found that the intensity of the black box really worked well. We had a 12 foot square stage. On the ground we taped out a spiders web. The actors stayed on stage throughout and our props and furniture were minimal.

The basic set 'imagined' the Brontës room in Haworth – a chaise longue at the back (the place Emily died) and basic chairs set to the sides, with writing slopes for each of the Brontës and a couple of 'treasure' chests which contained the moveable props. From here we took the audience on a range of fantastical adventures – from Haworth to the battefields of Waterloo – and to the fictional lands of Angria and Gondal.

The four actors played all the parts, doubling up the roles of Brontë created 'characters.' The changes were designated by different coloured sashes, cloaks and the use of wigs. The actors also 'aged' from children to adults over the course of the play. It is no surprise to note that we were not aiming at strict 'realism' in the production.

The Brontës wrote melodrama and the style of melodrama is, I suggest, the best angle of approach to staging. We are dealing for at least half the play with children 'playing' at being adults after all. In the second, darker half of the play we are delving into the psychological more deeply and the 'lines' of imagination are well drawn. There is more than realism to be enjoyed here.

It has to be said that melodrama works so much better on the stage than on the page, especially today. I still believe it to be a valid theatrical (and narrative) form, but much of the humour of young people 'aping' the melodramatic writing of their day is only really accessible when you watch actors in performance. This whole play is a work of the imagination – but the imagination stems primarily from the Brontës. What is required from directors and actors is a commitment to re-imagining the 'reality' while 'believing' in the many layered fantasy worlds they are presenting to the audience. When this succeeds the 'magic' of theatre allows for the audience to be transported from the 21st century through a small Haworth sitting room to the open battlefields of Waterloo – and beyond into the further reaches of the imagination. It's quite a journey.

ACT ONE SCENE ONE

We open to a black stage. Centre spotlight only lights Charlotte who stands in the middle of the central area which is marked out in tape with a spiders web.

CHARLOTTE: The busy day has hurried by, And hearts greet kindred hearts once more; And swift the evening hours should fly, But- what turns every gleaming eye, So often to the door.

Lights up to reveal DSR a trunk. DSL are two chairs either end of a trunk - these covered to give the impression of a chaise long. On this lies EMILY. Behind her stand BRANWELL and ANNE. USR two more trunks.

CHARLOTTE: And then so quick away - and why does sudden silence chill the room?

Emily is dying. Branwell holds her hand and Anne closes her eyes

CHARLOTTE: And laughter sink into a sigh, And merry words to whispers die, And gladness turn to gloom.

Emily, Branwell and Anne come to join Charlotte on their

15

respective lines - forming up to a tableau "the gun picture"

BRANWELL: Oh we are listening for a sound
EMILY: We know shall ne'er be heard again.
ANNE: Sweet voices in the halls resound
CHARLOTTE: Fair forms, fond faces gather round.
ALL: But all in vain - in vain!

Emily moves DSR to sit on the trunk.

EMILY: Their feet shall never waken more The echoes in these galleries wide,

Anne and Emily spread a cape centre stage - wave in the air as a mountain, then lay on the ground as a river.

EMILY: Nor dare the snow on the mountain's brow Nor skim the river's frozen flow, Nor wander down its side. They, they who have been our life - our soul - Through summer-youth, from childhood's spring
ANNE: Who bound us in one vigorous whole/
BRANWELL: /To stand 'gainst Tyranny's control, For ever triumphing.
ANNE: Who bore the brunt of battle's fray.
BRANWELL: The first to fight
They fight.

16

CHARLOTTE: The last to fall. Whose mighty minds

BRANWELL: With kindred ray.

CHARLOTTE: Still led the van in glory's way EMILY: The idol chiefs of all.

The fight is over.

EMILY: They, they are gone! Not for a while As golden suns at night decline,

CHARLOTTE: And even in death our grief beguile, Foretelling with a rose red smile, How bright the morn will shine.

EMILY: NO; these dark towers are lone and lorn; This very crowd is vacancy

CHARLOTTE: And we must watch, and wait, and mourn

ANNE: And half look out for their return

BRANWELL: And think their forms we see.

EMILY: And fancy music in our ear

ANNE: Such as their lips could only pour

BRANWELL: And think we feel their presence near

CHARLOTTE: And start to find they are not here

ALL: And never shall be more.

BLACKOUT

ACT ONE SCENE TWO

The parsonage, Haworth 1826. Charlotte, aged 10 sits DSL on one end of the chaise longue, writing in a notebook. Anne sits curled up at the chair at the end.

CHARLOTTE: Papa lent me this book. The book is an hundred and twenty years old. It is at this moment lying before me as I write this. I am in the kitchen of the parsonage house, Haworth. Tabby the servant is washing up after breakfast and Anne, my youngest sister (stern look) is kneeling on a chair, looking at some cakes which Tabby has been baking for us. Emily is in the parlour brushing the carpet. Papa and Branwell are gone to Keighly. Aunt is upstairs in her room and I am sitting by the table, writing this in the kitchen.

Branwell enters with a box of soldiers.

CHARLOTTE: When papa came home it was night and we were in bed, so next morning Branwell came to our door with a box of soldiers. Emily and I jumped out of bed and I snatched one up and exclaimed.

Charlotte and Emily run over to the box and take out a soldier each.

CHARLOTTE: This is the Duke of Wellington. It shall be mine!

She goes back to her writing. She is stage-managing the actions which follow.

CHARLOTTE: When I said this, Emily likewise took one and said it should be hers. When Anne came down, she took one also.

Charlotte is clearly impatient, as Anne, the youngest, is always one step behind in the game. The girls sit in the middle of the "web" to play with the soldiers. The spotlight moves to Branwell who is writing DSR.

BRANWELL: On June the fifth, AD eighteen twenty six, papa procured from Leeds another set of soldiers. I carried them to Emily, Charlotte and Anne. They each took up a soldier, gave them names, which I consented to, and I gave Charlotte Wellington, to Emily Gravey, or Parry, to Anne Waiting Boy, or Ross, to take care of them, though they were mine, and I to have disposal of them as I would.

He gathers up the soldiers. Anne slightly resistent to letting hers go. Branwell shows the girls his small booklet.

BRANWELL: What is contained in this history is a statement of what myself, Charlotte, Emily and Anne really pretended did happen.

The four children sit on the floor - playing a new game.

CHARLOTTE: We set sail with a fair wind from England on the first of March, seventeen ninety three. On the fifteenth we came in sight of Spain, On the sixteenth we landed, bought a supply of provisions (Emily picks a telescope out of the box.) and set sail again on the twentieth. On the twenty fifth, about noon, Henry Clinton who was in the shrouds, cried out that he saw the oxeye.

Anne grabs the telescope, rushes to the chaise longue, kneels on it, looking through the telescope.

ANNE: I see the oxeye.

The others look at her disparagingly. But the game is on, and they all act out their parts in the ensuing speech.

BRANWELL: In a minute we were on deck and all eyes gazing eagerly and fearfully towards the mountain over which we saw hanging in the sky the ominous speck. Instantly the sails were furled, and the boat was made

20

ready for launching in our last extremity. Thus having made everything ready we retired to the cabin; everyone looked as sheepish as possible, and in no way inclined to meet our fate like men.

Anne is carried away by the game, and begins to cry.

BRANWELL: Some of us began to cry

Emily comforts her and throws dagger looks at Branwell to tone the story down.

BRANWELL: But we waited a long time and heard no sound of the wind and the cloud did not increase in size. At last Marcus O'Donnel exclaimed.
EMILY: I wish it would either go backward or forward.
BRANWELL: At this he received a box on the ear.

Charlotte boxes Emily's ear. Emily retaliates.

BRANWELL: O'Donnel returned the compliment.

The tussle looks like it's getting out of hand, so Branwell intervenes, reminding them it's HIS story.

BRANWELL: But just then we heard the sound of the wind

and Henry bawled out.

Proud that Branwell is including her again, Anne plays her part to the full again...

ANNE: The cloud is as big as me!

Another stern look from big brother not to overdo it. Branwell senses he's losing control of the story.

BRANWELL: We were all silenced by a fierce flash of lightening and a loud peal of thunder. The wind rose and the planks of our ship creaked. Another flash of lightening, brighter and more terrible than the first, split our mainmast and carried away our topsail. And now the flashes of lightening grew terrific and the thunder roared tremendously. The rain poured down in torrents and the gusts of wind were most loud and terrible. The hearts of the stoutest men in our company now quailed.

Branwell has got totally carried away. Charlotte is determined to take control once more. She challenges him.

CHARLOTTE: At last the storm ceased. *(pause)* But we found it had driven us quite out of our course and we knew not where we were. When we spied land, we sailed

22

along the coast for some time to find a good landing place. To our surprise we found the country cultivated.

EMILY: Grain of a peculiar sort grew in great abundance.

BRANWELL: And there were large plantations of palm trees.

ANNE: There were also many olives, and large enclosures of rice.

The others throw her a withering look - be real in your fantasy!

CHARLOTTE: We were greatly surprised at these marks of the land being inhabited.

The children prepare for the new game. Charlotte and Branwell arm with swords and sashes. Emily and Anne are the natives.

BRANWELL: After we had travelled about two miles, we saw at a distance twenty men, armed.

Emily and Anne stand firm, armed to the teeth with a shelalagh and a broom.

BRANWELL: We immediately prepared for battle, having each of us sword, musket and bayonet.

He picks up toy muskets from the toy chest USC and throws one to Charlotte. Then he brandishes his at the "enemy"

CHARLOTTE: We stood still and they came near.

Emily and Anne seem disinclined to come too near to the weapons. But Charlotte is in charge of the game and they are persuaded.

BRANWELL: When they had come close up to us, they likewise stopped. They seemed greatly surprised.

Anne holds her ground, Emily walks round Branwell and Charlotte.

ANNE: What strange people.
EMILY: Who are you? (*as if confused as to who everyone is in the game*)
CHARLOTTE: We were cast up on your shores by a storm and request shelter.
ANNE/EMILY: You shall not have it.
CHARLOTTE: We will take it then.

They fight. Ending in the capture, at sword point, of Emily the chief and the retreat of Anne.
BRANWELL: It was a very fierce encounter but we

24

conquered. Killed ten, took the chief prisoner, wounded five and the remaining four retreated.

He holds Emily at sword point.

BRANWELL: The chief was quite black, very tall. He had a fierce countenance and the finest eyes I ever saw. We asked him what his name was...

Emily stands stock still.

BRANWELL: But he would not speak.

Branwell looks to Charlotte for support - make her do what I say!

BRANWELL: We asked him...
CHARLOTTE: Then what is the name of your country?

Emily still doesn't seem to be playing. Branwell pushes the point.

BRANWELL: And he said...

After a considered pause, when she has made the point that she's in charge of at least her part of the story, Emily answers with all the authority of an African chief.

EMILY: Ashantee.

Branwell and Charlotte are happy that the game can now continue. They include Anne, who acts out her part in the following speech.

BRANWELL: Next morning a party of twelve men came to our tents, bringing with them a ransom for their chief and likewise a proposition of peace from their king.

Anne offers them toys.

BRANWELL: This we accepted, as it was on terms most advantageous to ourselves. Then we set about building ourselves a city.

BLACKOUT

ACT ONE SCENE THREE

*An adult Anne (1850) is sitting writing about the past -
Charlotte and Branwell as children are dressing for their
parts.*

ANNE: Charlotte and Branwell established the imaginary
world of Angria. Emily and I only joined in to swell the
numbers, and the main characters became firmly
established. Charlotte was Arthur Wellesley, the eldest son
of the Duke of Wellington, who became in later days
Marquis of Douro and Duke of Zamorna. Branwell was
Alexander Rogue, or Percy, Lord Ellrington and Duke of
Northangerland. There were many bitter rivalries between
these characters over a span of nearly ten years. The first
disagreement leads to the Great Rebellion of eighteen thirty
one.

Emily sits beside Anne, also writing at her slope.

EMILY: I moved from the world of Angria to the world of
Gondal, a secret world shared only between Anne and
myself. But we still played our role in Angria. We were
useful as backdrops to the more exciting characters of
Douro and Rogue.

Branwell is dressed and ready for another game. The others will follow the actions he narrates.

BRANWELL: One evening about dusk, as the Marquis Douro was returning from a shooting excursion into the country, he heard suddenly a rustling noise in a deep ditch on the roadside. He was preparing his fowling piece for a shot, when the form of Lady Ellrington *(played by Emily)* started up before him. Her head was bare, her tall person was enveloped in the tattered remnants of a dark velvet mantle. Her dishevelled hair hung in wild elflocks over her face, neck and shoulders, almost concealing her features, which were emaciated and pale as death. He stepped back a few paces, startled at the sudden and ghastly apparition. She threw herself on her knees before him, exclaiming in wild, maniacal accents

EMILY: *(as Lady Ellrington)* My lord. Tell me, truly, sincerely, ingenuously, where you have been. I heard that you had left Verdopolis, and I followed you on foot five hundred miles. Then my strength failed me, and I lay down in this place, as I thought to die. But I was doomed I should see you once more before I became an inhabitant of the grave. Answer me, my lord. Have you seen that wretch Marian Hume? Have you spoken to her. Viper! Viper! Oh that I could sheathe this weapon in her heart.

28

Emily pulls out a quill pen, masquerading as a knife. She is getting truly carried away and Branwell steps in to take back control of the story.

BRANWELL: Here she stopped for want of breath.

Emily gives him a dirty look. He relents somewhat.

BRANWELL: And drawing a long, sharp, glittering knife from under her cloak, brandished it wildly in the air. The Marquis looked at her steadily, and without attempting to disarm her, answered with great composure.

CHARLOTTE: (*As Douro*) You have asked me a strange question Lady Zenobia, but before I attempt to answer it, you had better come with me to our encampment. I will order a tent to be prepared for you where you may pass the night in safety and tomorrow, when you are a little recruited by rest and refreshment, we will discuss this matter soberly.

BRANWELL: Her rage was now exhausted by its own vehemence and she replied with more calmness than she had hitherto evinced.

EMILY:(*as Zenobia*) My lord, believe me, I am deputed by heaven to warn you of a great danger into which you are about to fall. If you persist in your intention of uniting yourself to Marian Hume, you will become a murderer and a suicide. I cannot now explain myself more clearly; but ponder carefully on my words until I see you again.

BRANWELL: Then bowing her forehead to the earth in an attitude of adoration, she kissed his feet, muttering at the same time some unintelligible words. The Marquis paced slowly back to camp, lost in deep reflection on what he had heard and seen.

ANNE: Months rolled away and the mystery remained unsolved. Lady Zenobia Ellrington appeared as usual. Her voice was more subdued and her looks pale, and it was remarked by some that she avoided all communication with the Marquis.

BRANWELL: In the meantime, the Duke of Wellington had consented to his son's union with the beautiful, virtuous, and accomplished, but untitled, Marian Hume.

Charlotte and Anne prepare for their roles. Once again, Anne gets above herself enjoying the veil and Branwell is barbed in his comment "untitled."

BRANWELL: Vast and splendid preparations were in the making for the approaching bridal, when just at this critical juncture news arrives of the Great Rebellion headed by Alexander Rogue.

He's seen that the girls are all getting too into the "wedding" part of the story, wants to reinsert some "action."

BRANWELL: Unequivocal symptoms of dissatisfaction began to appear among the lower orders in Verdopolis. The workmen at the principal mills and furnaces struck for an advance in wages. Colonel Grenville, one of the great mill-owners, was shot. His assassins were interrogated by torture, but they remained inflexible, not a single satisfactory answer being elicited from them. Orders were issued that no citizen should walk abroad unarmed. Parliament was summoned to consult on the best measures to be taken. In the house, the Marquis of Douro rose and made one of his most celebrated orations.

CHARLOTTE: (*as Douro*) I call on you, my countrymen, to rouse yourselves to action. There is a latent flame of rebellion smouldering in our city, which blood alone can quench: the hot blood of ourselves and our enemies freely poured forth. We daily see in our streets, men whose brows were once open as the day, but which are now wrinkled with dark dissatisfaction, and the light of whose eyes, formerly free as sunshine, is now dimmed by restless suspicion. Our peaceful citizens cannot pass their thresh-holds in safety unless laded with weapons of war, the continual dread of death haunting their footsteps wherever they turn. And who has produced this awful change? What agency of hell has effected, what master spirit of crime,

31

what prince of sin, what Beelzebub of black iniquity has been at work in the kingdom? I will answer that fearful question: Alexander Rogue! Arm for the battle then, fellow countrymen; be not faint-hearted , but trust in the justice of your cause as your banner of protection and let your war shout in the onslaught ever be "God defend the right".

ANNE: When the Marquis had finished this harangue, he left the house amidst long and thunderous applause, and proceeded to a shady grove on the river banks. There he came across Zenobia.

EMILY: (*as Zenobia*) My lord, your eloquence, your noble genius has again driven me to desperation. I am no longer mistress of myself, and if you do not consent to be mine and mine alone, I will kill myself where I stand.

CHARLOTTE: (*As Douro*) Lady Ellrington, this conduct is unworthy of your character. I must beg that you will cease to use the language of a madwoman, for, I do assure you, my lady, these deep stratagems will have no effect on me.

EMILY: (*as Zenobia*) Oh! Do not kill me with such cold cruel disdain. Only consent to follow me, and you will be utterly convinced that you ought not to be united to one so utterly unworthy of you as Marian Hume.

Douro follows Zenobia.

EMILY: (as Zenobia) You are now in the sacred presence of

one whose counsel I am sure you, my lord, will never slight.

Branwell is hidden USL under a cloak. He is playing the part of an oracle.

BRANWELL: Hearken to the counsels of wisdom and do not in the madness of self will, destroy yourself and Marian Hume, by refusing the offered hand of one whom, from the moment of your birth was doomed by the prophetic stars of heaven to be your partner and support through the dark, unexplored wilderness of future life.

Anne cannot stand the excitement. She whispers into Charlotte's ear.

ANNE: There is danger, beware.

Branwell reveals himself as Rogue.

EMILY: About a week after this event the nuptials of Arthur Augustus, Marquis of Douro, and Marian Hume, were solemnized.

They act out the marriage.

BRANWELL: After a time, Lady Ellrington seemed to recover, and the Marquis, convinced that her extravagances had arisen from a disordered brain, consented to honour her with his friendship once more.

CHARLOTTE: But Zenobia sought revenge on Arthur, by marrying his rival, Alexander Rogue. She was still madly in love with the Marquis and thus their marriage was not destined for success.

EMILY: (*as Zenobia*) Oh, that I should have resigned myself into the hands of such a man, in a moment of pique at love neglected, contemned, spurned; in an hour of false, fleeting admiration of abused and degraded talents. I yielded up my liberty and received the galling yoke of worse than Egyptian bondage. Arthur. Arthur! Why did I ever see you? Why did I ever hear your voice? If love for another did not occupy my whole heart, absorb my whole existence, perhaps I might endure the cruelty of this man with less utter, less unendurable misery. Perhaps I might, by unwearied patience, by constant and tender submission, win some portion of his regard, some slight share of his affection. But now it is impossible. I cannot love him. I cannot even appear to love him, and therefore I must hereafter drag out the remnant of my wretched life in sorrow and woe, in hopeless and careless mourning.

BRANWELL: (*as Rogue*) Well, termagent. I suppose you thought I'd forgotten your insolent behaviour to me about a week ago, but I assure you if that was our opinion you're very much mistaken. Kneel at my feet this instant and humbly and submissively ask pardon for all past offences or...

He grabs her arm. She pushes him off.

EMILY: (*as Zenobia*) Never, never will I so far degrade myself. Do not hope, do not imagine that I will.

He draws a sword.

BRANWELL: (*as Rogue*) I neither hope nor imagine anything about the matter, but I'm certain of it; at least if you refuse, an inch of cold steel will find it's way to your heart. Do you think that I will have you dancing and manoeuvring before my very face with that conceited, impertinent, white livered puppy.

EMILY: (*as Zenobia*) Dare not, at your peril, to speak another insulting word of the the Marquis of Douro.

BRANWELL: (*as Rogue*) Fool and madwoman. Is this the language calculated to screen either you or him from the terrible effects of my wrath? You may grovel now in the dust. You may kneel and implore my forgiveness till your bold tongue rots and refuses to move. I will not grant it now were ever angel celestial and infernal to command me.

EMILY: (*as Zenobia*) Base villain, I scorn your forgiveness. I trample your offers of mercy underfoot. And think not to harm the Marquis, he is far above your power. That blood-stained, that crime-blackened hand, could not harm one hair of his noble head. Yet know, wretch, that though I honour him thus highly, though I look upon him as more than a man, as an angel, a demigod, yet - rather than break my faith even with you, I would this instant fall a corpse at your feet.

BRANWELL: (*as Rogue*) Liar. These words shall be your sentence and I will execute quickly. But you shall not die quickly. No! I'll thrust this sharp blade slowly through you that you may feel and enjoy the torture.

They fight.

CHARLOTTE: He twisted his hand in her thick black hair, and was just in the act of striking her as she lay, unresisting and motionless, when a strong and sudden grasp arrested his arm from behind. Half choked with fury, he turned round to see the hideous visage of Montmorency.

ANNE: (a reluctant *Montmorency*) My beloved friend, in passing I happened to look through your keyhole, and I beheld as pretty a tragedy as one could wish to set eyes on, but when I saw that matters were approaching a crisis, I

36

remembered that the gallows often follows murder. Thus I stepped forward like a hero, and effected the deliverance of this fair damsel in distress.

BRANWELL: (*as Rogue*) Well, since the brother of my heart has interposed, I will permit that woman to escape the punishment due to her crimes this once. (To Emily) Get up you heap of baseness and begone instantly from my presence.

BLACKOUT

ACT TWO SCENE ONE

CHARLOTTE: Storms are waking to inspire us

BRANWELL: Storms upon our morning sky.

EMILY: Wildly wailing tempests fire us.

ANNE: With their loud, God-given cry.

CHARLOTTE: Winds, our trumpets, shrieking come

BRANWELL: Thundering waves our deeper drum

EMILY/ANNE: Wild woods o'er us, swell the chorus Bursting on the starry gloom.

CHARLOTTE: What's their omen?

BRANWELL: Whence the doom?

CHARLOTTE: Storms are waking

BRANWELL: Earth is shaking

EMILY: Banners wave and bugles wail.

ANNE: And beneath the tempest breaking, Some must quiver/

EMILY: /Some must quail.

BRANWELL: Hark the artillery's iron hail, Rattles through the ranks of war, Who beneath its force shall fail?

CHARLOTTE: Tempest blow thy mightiest blast

EMILY: Wild wind sound thy wildest strain

ANNE: From God's right hand, O'er his chosen land, Your music shall waken its fires again.

CHARLOTTE: And over the north now

EMILY: And over the ocean

ANNE: And whoever shall shadow these storm covered skies.

BRANWELL: The louder though battle may roar

ALL: 'Twill only sound stronger - OH ANGRIA - ARISE!

BLACKOUT

ACT TWO SCENE TWO

ANNE: (*As Edward*) And this is Verdopolis. That splendid city, rising with such graceful haughtiness from the green realm of Neptune. Queen of nations, accept the homage of one who seeks but to be among the number of thy slaves!

EMILY: Such was Edward Sydney's brief, but enthusiastic address to our beloved city as he caught the first glimpse of her proud enduring towers. As he rested from his travels at Bravey's hotel, a wagon appeared, followed by a troop of musicians and some ragged looking children.

BRANWELL: (*as Rogue)* Gentlemen, we are now going to show you a feat which never has been performed before and never will be again.

EMILY: What followed was the most horrible sight. Edward was forced to watch as the two children were set to dancing within the flames of a fire, until they were completely consumed by it. He watched with feelings of such deep horror as rendered him unable to stir, but at length he rushed forward from the crowd.

ANNE: (*as Edward*) Wretch! How dare you thus brutally murder innocent children in the open street, and how gentlemen... How can you behold such infernal barbarity unmoved.

CHARLOTTE: (*as Douro*) What is the matter?

BRANWELL: (*as Rogue*) Nothing but an Englishman

41

singing over his deserts.

CHARLOTTE: (*as Douro*) Hold your teeth you scoundrel. I'll knock your teeth down your throat if I hear any more impudence. Deliver up your prey on pain of death.

She draws a sword. Threatens Branwell. Then turns to Anne.

CHARLOTTE: I should like to know what brought you into such a pickle.

ANNE: (*as Edward*) I merely attempted to remonstrate with that horrible monster, respecting his treatment of some innocent children whom he was cruelly murdering.

BRANWELL: (*as Rogue*) A stuck pig. Meddling ninny. Come now Douro, you surely won't spend any more time in talking to such a whey faced whiner?

CHARLOTTE: (*as Douro*) Hold your tongue or else bite it off!

CHARLOTTE: (To Anne)I want to know sir, where this unhappy heap of mortality is going. I say Sir. In what direction will you turn your charming phiz now? You look very much in doubt as to the matter I can say.

ANNE: (*as Edward*) Really sir, I do not know what right you have to ask me such a question.

CHARLOTTE: *(as Douro)* The right of might.

Turns her sword on Anne.

CHARLOTTE: (*as Douro*) Come my lad, you and I must not part in this way. I see by that flash in your eye that you're worth preserving.

ANNE: (*as Edward*) Sir, I will not be detained.

There is a brief fight. Which Charlotte wins hands down.

CHARLOTTE: (*as Douro*) But you shall Sir, and that as long as I please.

EMILY: Edward was kept confined by the Marquis for two weeks. On the fifteenth morning, as he pensively entered the library, he started on perceiving Douro seated at the breakfast table and engaged in perusing a newspaper. As Edward came forward, Douro rose, and advanced to meet him with that bewitching smile which he so well knows how to assume, and frankly offering his hand, addressed him thus.

CHARLOTTE: (*as Douro*) Well my good fellow, I am at last come to set you free. Nothing, I assure you, but the most urgent business could have prevented me from visiting you long since, and I did not choose to send orders for your release, because, as you are an Englishman, and totally unacquainted with the manners of our citizens, I knew that you would be continually getting into scrapes, some of which might have proved fatal to you before assistance

43

could be procured. I have no desire to detain you any longer against your inclination, but before you go, permit me to ask a few questions. In the first place, what is your name?

ANNE: (as Edward) Edward Sydney.

CHARLOTTE: (as Douro) Are you possessed of an independent fortune?

ANNE: (as Edward) My income amounts to three thousand pounds per annum.

CHARLOTTE: (as Douro) Is it derived from landed property or commercial concerns?

ANNE: (as Edward) From landed property.

CHARLOTTE: (as Douro) Are you parents living? ANNE: (as Edward) I don't know.

CHARLOTTE: (as Douro) How have you been brought up?

ANNE: (as Edward) I have received a University education.

CHARLOTTE: (as Douro) Which I presume from your juvenile appearance is not yet completed?

ANNE: (as Edward) Yes it is. I attained the rank of senior wrangler, and took my degree before I left College.

CHARLOTTE: Senior wrangler! Why? What age are you?

ANNE: Twenty two.

EMILY: A slight blush suffused the young nobleman's fine features at this reply. He answered quickly.

CHARLOTTE: (as Douro) Why, I have been conversing with you all this time as if you were my junior, and now it turns out that I am myself three years younger than you.

ANNE: (*as Edward*) Do not be offended my lord, your superior stature and manliness of bearing are sufficient excuses for the mistake.

CHARLOTTE: (*as Douro*) Well, never mind. I have taken upon myself the office of patron, and I will maintain it were you fifty years my senior. Now pray tell me if you would like to be a member of the Commons House of Parliament which represents this great Empire?

ANNE: *(as Edward)* My lord, are you in earnest?

CHARLOTTE: (*as Douro*) Decidedly so.

ANNE: (*as Edward*) Then nothing would be more gratifying to every feeling of my heart.

CHARLOTTE: (*as Douro*) You would consider that a lucky event which should elevate you to such a post?

ANNE: (*as Edward*) The most superlatively so of any that ever happened to me.

CHARLOTTE: (*as Douro*) Then know, Mr Sydney, that the business in which I have been engaged during the last fortnight, was ousting an obnoxious member from his seat, and procuring your election instead. But now, do you know what is required of you as a return for this piece of service?

ANNE: (*as Edward*) I believe I do.

CHARLOTTE: (*as Douro*) What?

ANNE: (*as Edward*) A staunch and unflinching opposition

to the vile demagogue Alexander Rogue.

CHARLOTTE: (*as Douro*) You have hit the nail right on the head.

BLACKOUT

EMILY: A grand ball and supper was held by the Major General Lord Selby. Douro and Marian, Rogue and Zenobia were all invited.

BRANWELL: It was the last function they both attended before the Great Rebellion started and Angria was plunged into bloody and bitter civil war.

CHARLOTTE: (*as Douro*) Marian, what is the matter sir? What were you saying to this lady?

BRANWELL: (*as Rogue*) I do not know whether I am obliged to tell you everything I say to such ladies as I choose to honour with my notice.

CHARLOTTE: (*as Douro*) But you shall tell me or..

ANNE: (*as Marian*) Arthur, Arthur, don't be so angry. He was only asking me to dance and I was so silly as to turn away without replying and that displeased him I suppose.

BRANWELL: (*as Rogue*) No fair lady, it did not displease me, but I trust you will now grant me a favourable answer?

ANNE: (*as Marian*) Sir, I hope you will excuse me when I say that I cannot comply with your request.

BRANWELL: (*as Rogue*) And why not?

ANNE: (*as Marian*) Because I do not think my husband's enemy a fit companion for myself. BRANWELL: (as Rogue) Oh! If that is your only objection, I do not despair.

He turns to Emily.

47

BRANWELL: (*as Rogue*) Madam, prepare instantly to quit this place and to proceed homewards.

EMILY: (*as Zenobia*) Three hours hence I will do so, but not till then.

BRANWELL: (*as Rogue*) What! Am I to be bearded in this way by my own wife? Obey my commands this instant or I shall find some method of compelling you to your duty.

EMILY: (*as Zenobia*) Ellrington, I know your motives for acting thus, but be assured I will never succumb to such unjust, such tyrannical treatment. You are sensible that once my determination is fixed it seldom alters, therefore give yourself no further trouble, for I will not go home - yet.

Branwell goes back to his seat - annoyed. Emily joins Charlotte and Anne, in the dance.

EMILY: (*as Zenobia*) Well my lord, I suppose it is as much your fault as mine that we do not see each other oftener. Why do you never come to Ellrington House?

CHARLOTTE: (*as Douro*) Why, my lady, surely you would not wish me to frequent the house of a man whom I detest and who detests me?

EMILY: (*as Zenobia*) Sir, it is not my husband's residence, it is mine, and there I will see any visitors I please without asking his leave.

CHARLOTTE: (*as Douro*) I will not dispute your ladyship's

48

resolution, which doubtless is perfectly just, but as I have no inclination to involve either you or myself in unnecessary fracas with your worthy husband, you will excuse me when I say that I should prefer meeting you in the house of a third person rather than in your own house. Now let us change the subject. What makes you so melancholy and so fond of solitude now? In former times you were the life and soul of every party that was so fortunate to be honoured by your presence.

EMILY: (*as Zenobia*) Arthur. That question sounds rather taunting. How can I be otherwise than melancholy when I am united for life to a tyrant, and what pleasure can I find in society where my best and dearest friends regard me with coldness and suspicion because I am the unwilling wife of a demagogue.

CHARLOTTE: (*as Douro*) Yes, but Zenobia, I once thought you had a spirit which would rise superior to all terrestrial evils, and now you tremble at the frown of a wretch who is scarcely worthy to be your vassal.

EMILY: (*as Zenobia*) Arthur. You do not know Rogue. His anger once roused is terrible, unappeasable. I have often striven to stand against it, but in vain. He always compels me to abject submission in spite of that spirit which you used to call unconquerable.

CHARLOTTE: *(as Douro)* Yet you withstood him bravely tonight my lady.

49

EMILY: (*as Zenobia*) I did. But it was your presence gave me courage. I resolved that you at least should not see me cowed and degraded by him. But when we return home I shall have to pay the penalty for my steadfastness and a heavy one it will be.

ANNE: (*as Marian*) I pity you very much my lady, but at the same time I feel very glad that I am not married to such a hideous and cruel man.

EMILY: I give you envy in return for your pity.

CHARLOTTE: (*as Douro*) Marian. How dare you call Lord Ellrington hideous. (*as herself*) He is a very handsome man in my opinion.

ANNE: He is not so in mine though. (*as Marian*) His very look frightened me so far from my propriety that I could not muster sufficient sense to frame an answer to his question.

CHARLOTTE: Why you little carping critic. What particular features in his face do you find fault with?

ANNE: His eyes I think, though I can't say with exactness, where all are so ugly.

CHARLOTTE: His eyes! They are as fine dark optics as any one could wish to see.

ANNE: That does not signify. They are totally unlike yours, not so large, not so bright, not so smiling and therefore I hate them.

EMILY: And so do I.   BLACKOUT

ANNE: It was night. The clocks had all chimed twelve. The saloons were fireless and lampless. No company had enlivened them that night or for many preceeding ones. Rogue had disappeared months before, taking with him his mistress, Louisa Vernon.

Emily, as Zenobia - a Victorian melodramatic heroine verging on Lady MacBeth, glides slowly across the stage.

CHARLOTTE: Zenobia, as she glided past their portals thought how lonely their silence and darkness was. With a less inceding and slower tread than was customary to her, she sought her chamber with the intention of retiring to rest, for she was weary of struggling against thoughts that tamed her pride and lowered her soaring spirits.

ANNE: A fine woman she looked with a solemn but not sad aspect in her eyes as she opened the door and crossed the threshold of her dressing room. Why does she stop? What means that look of astonishment, changing quickly into one of a different and inscrutable meaning, that parting of the beautiful lips and that sudden erection of the splendid bust.

CHARLOTTE: A tall shadow quivers on the walls and ceiling. Look, yonder! That is a human being, a man, a gentleman! Yes, one in a black dress with a white forehead and fine nose leans against that cabinet with folded arms and eyes directed straight, daringly and unflinchingly towards the awful Countess. The first petrifying effect of this apparition over, Zenobia closed the door.

ANNE: In a moment she turned and glanced again on the intruder as if to be certain he was still there; he was indeed but he had changed his place and stood close beside her.

EMILY: *(as Zenobia)* Rogue.

BRANWELL: *(as Rogue)* Why my dear Zenobia, this excitement makes you look interesting, almost so much so as... as... Louisa Vernon.

EMILY: *(as Zenobia)* My lord. I am a Western! And the heiress of Henry Ellrington of Ennerdale, and the granddaughter of Don John Louisiada. I will not be insulted - by my life. I would have forgiven you and loved you again at that moment because you looked pale and weary, but I'll not now. You did ill to speak of Louisa Vernon - I thought you were tired of your false rest and come back to lean upon your true one in adversity.

BRANWELL: *(as Rogue)* I am, my Countess, and a most placid rest I've found. You look all repose Zenobia.

EMILY: *(as Zenobia)* You are possessed. You are sick at heart I see, and satiated, and utterly without hope, and yet there's a light foam on your desperation that churns up the more wantonly and fantastically the more madly the torrent rushes.

BRANWELL: (*as Rogue*) An Evangelical truth! Verily your ladyship speaks right. Satiated I was with the semi-gallic, semi-Italian and wholly Paradisaical graces of my delightful Louisa, ennui utterly by her grasping monopoly of my precious self and her tiresome jealousy of my favours.

Frightened at her violence and propensity to scenes. I began to look for the dying scene as a relief but it never came. I took myself off. I wandered here and there, and when I'm at last arrived, after an absence as they say in the newspapers of nearly three months, my wife's first greeting is couched in a genealogical account of herself and her family. Talking of those times reminds me of one Alexander Rogue that I used to know. It's long since and I remember very little about him except that his brains were less irretrievably cracked than those of the present, most mighty Earl of Northangerland.

Zenobia! What did that glance mean? It meant you thought me mad. You are frightened at hearing my jaunty desperation! I don't pretend to say I've lost my senses, or that I'm much wronged or in frenzied despair, to speak the truth, I'm only horribly dissatisfied.

EMILY: Then lash your broken, helmless bark wholly to me. I've enough firmness and fidelity to be a most steadfast anchor. Trust me!

BRANWELL: That is to say, in other words, tie yourself to my apron strings. I might have yielded, but another thought has just struck me. There's one quarter I've left untried. A project has entered my head, shabby, despicable, and contemptible in its nature and therefore the more in harmony with the whole state of my feelings. Good night, Zenobia.

BLACKOUT

ACT TWO SCENE FIVE

BRANWELL: Welcome heroes to the war, Welcome to your glory. Will you seize your swords and dare, To be renowned in story?

EMILY: What though fame be distant far, Flashing through the upper air. Though the path which leads you there, Be long and rough and gory?

ANNE: Angrians, when your morning rose, Before your monarch's eye, He swore that ere it's evening close, All your foes should fly.

CHARLOTTE: Down from heaven Zamorna came, To guide you to the sky, And shook his sword of quenchless flame And shouted VICTORY!

BRANWELL: Angrians, if your noble king, Rides foremost in the fight, Up in glorious gathering Around that helmet bright.

CHARLOTTE: Angrians, if you wield your sword,

Every stroke shall be, Fixed as one undying word, In Afric's history.

EMILY:Angrians if in fight you die, The clouds that o'er you rise, Shall waft your spirits to a sky, Of everlasting joy.

ANNE: Angrians, when that fight is o'er, Heaven and earth and sea, Shall echo in the Cannon's roar, Your shout of victory.

CHARLOTTE: So now if all your bosoms beat

ANNE: To reach your native star

EMILY: Shake the shackles from your feet.

BRANWELL: And welcome to the WAR!

They fight.

BLACKOUT

CHARLOTTE: Time has passed. Marian Hume died an untimely death, and Douro married Rogue's daughter Mary. He hoped by this to turn an enemy into a friend. Douro became Duke of Zamorna and Rogue became Earl of Northangerland. An uneasy peace reigns until Zamorna inherits the crown of Angria.

BRANWELL: It is time for Northangerland's revenge and he plots civil war.

CHARLOTTE: Zamorna swore that if he ever did this, his daughter Mary, now Queen of Angria, would suffer.

ANNE: The eyes of everyone are now open to the fact that our country Angria has just entered upon what will probably prove one of the most terrific intestine wars that have ever desolated the world. We know this because we see the fiery and daring characters of our people, the embroiled and exasperated state of parties, and above all, the bold, mighty and remarkable men who at present act as their leaders. Our eyes must first turn to Zamorna, who is in conference with his advisor, Howard Warner.

Branwell is in disguise as Warner.

BRANWELL: (*as Warner*) My lord - are you doing right? The matter lies between god and your own conscience. I know

57

that the kingdom must be saved at any hazard of individual peace or even life. I advocate expediency my lord. In the government of a state I allow of equivocal means to procure a just end. I sanction the shedding of blood and the cutting up of domestic happiness by the

roots to stab a traitor to the heart. But nevertheless, I am a man, sire, and after what I have seen during the last day or two, I ask your Majesty with solemn earnestness, is there no way by which the heart of Northangerland may be reached except through the breast of my Queen?

CHARLOTTE: *(as Zamorna)* Warner! But two living creatures in the world know of the nature of the relations that have existed between Alexander Rogue and myself. From the very beginning in my inmost soul, while I watched his devious and eccentric course, I swore that if he broke those bonds and so turned to vanity and scattered in the air sacrifices that I had made, and words that I had spoken, if he made as dust and nothingness causes for which I have endured jealousies and burning strife and emulations amongst those I loved; if he froze feelings that in me are like living fire, I would have revenge. In all but one quarter he is fortified and garrisoned. He can bid me defiance, but one quarter lies open to my javelin, and dipped in venom I will launch it quivering into his very spirit, so help me Hell!

BRANWELL: *(as Warner)* Hell will help you and I fear my

lord, God will veil his spirit that it will finally leave us. I am incessantly haunted by the certain knowledge that you, a man who has his reward in Earth in superior gifts and more splendid endowments than other men, that you have no place among the elect of god. Long before the foundations of the world were laid, you were numbered with the everlastingly condemned; all your thoughts and your words, the whole bent of your mind prove it. When you die Sire, and you are not framed for a long life, I shall bid you an eternal farewell. Your pulse once at rest we shall never meet again. There is a lady in the next room wishes to see you. May I admit her?

CHARLOTTE: (*as Zamorna*) As you like.

Emily approaches, disguised as Mary.

CHARLOTTE: (*as Zamorna*) Be so kind as to remove your veil madam.

EMILY: (*as Mary*) Sire, I want your Majesty's gracious permission to see my dear, dear husband once more in this world before he leaves me forever.

CHARLOTTE: (*as Zamorna*) Warner!

Branwell reveals himself under his disguise.

CHARLOTTE: (*as Zamorna*)Rogue! How dared you do what

you have done? How dared you bring my wife here, when you know I'd rather have an evil spirit given to my arms this night? You must have been conscious Sir, that I had wrought my resolution with toil and trouble. That I had decided to let her die, if her father cut loose, and decided with agony. (*Charlotte continues as herself showing Branwell her complete despair at his version of the 'story.'*): And what possessed you to ruin it all, and set me the whole torturing task over again.

Anne and Emily can see the direction things are taking and stay in the fantasy, acting as choric voices. This is less a reluctance to let the story die, and more a means of supporting Charlotte.

ANNE: The sword is drawn. The arm uplifted in the space that will intervene before the impending blow falls. Let Zamorna listen to the voice of his shuddering country. We will faithfully speak what she breathes in the hour of suspense, her head on the block and the executioners axe hanging over it.

EMILY: Sovereign! I was fair and flourishing, the happy Province of a mighty mother state. You saw me and I kindled your ambition - though the apparent heir to another throne, you would not wait till Death should take the diadem from your father's brows. You built a capital, you raised towns, you encouraged commerce, you modelled an army, you made me splendid without; I was gilded by your hand from the crown of my head to the sole of me foot. To attain this magnificence I was laden with debt.

ANNE: Now Zamorna. You should have been my mantle and my shield, and helmet for my head and a buckler for my bosom. You should have been my protector, my warder, my counsellor. Have you been this? Where is my capital? Beseiged, stormed, taken, a broken wall. Where are the men who supported me, where are their labours? All shattered, overthrown, involved in the general wreck of the Kingdom. Lastly, where is my army? I see it, there it stands, dispirited, enfeebled, wasted by disease and defeat, still rallying round your banner, still devoted to your cause, still obedient without murmur or mutiny to him for whose sake their homes are as lifeless and desolate as the fanes of the Indians in Peru.

EMILY: Still willing to present even life as their last sacrifice in his service, their last stake in the bloody game playing on his account. Waiting patiently, valiantly, to hear the word from your lips which shall send them to destruction or to a gory victory. Pause a moment Zamorna. Should that first event rush on them without hope of the last, should the reprieve delay and the axe descend, how will you feel as my blood streams over the scaffold? For my

61

part, I, yes I your martyred Angria, will curse you with my dying breath. I will curse you for your rashness, your cruelty, your selfishness, for the mean atrocity of hazarding a nation and the wealth of a nation. I shall despise you, and hate you and so will my children and their children to the third and fourth generation.

ANNE: You thought to be called the founder of a dynasty that should rule half the world. If tomorrow fate should prove adverse, you will be called the impious fool who aimed at Heaven, slipped and fell into Hell.

BLACKOUT

ACT TWO SCENE SEVEN

ANNE: As Northangerland sat at his breakfast preparing for the final rout of Zamorna, he received an unexpected visitor in the frame of his mother.

Charlotte and Branwell appear to have fully embraced their fictional roles at this point. This may be psychologically significant of things to come. There are things they cannot say to each other in reality.

MOTHER: (Charlotte) Alexander, what is this you are bent upon? Is it what I dread to name, and must I again see my son the curse not only of himself but of his country? I saw you raise the rebellion of 1832 and then you narrowly escaped death by the confiscation of a noble fortune. Will you tread the same ground over again, or Alexander, is it untrue, this frightful...

NORTHANGERLAND: *(Branwell)* True, madam, every inch of it – every word and letter.

MOTHER: (*Charlotte*) I cannot change you, I see. But I must wait calmly as I have by this time learned calmness from necessity. Alexander, is it your intention to throw this city into horrible confusion and ruin the ancient order of things?

NORTHANGERLAND: (*Branwell*) In six hours your

ladyship.

MOTHER:(*Charlotte*) I have borne long with you, my son, through years of unceasing vicissitudes; I have seen you a murderer, and outlaw, a rebel and now I see you without one single friend. And I – I feel my affection for you as if a guilty one, as if a crime to my country. You know Alexander, that my character is one which clings most firmly to one I love, through good report and evil report, sacrificing everything to the object of my affection. But there is a point beyond which I dare not go. Alexander, I once hoped that I should not have to detest you as a monster. But I know I cannot swerve you from your purpose. I have visited you because your daughter is dying. She saw that reconciliation between yourself and her husband was humanly impossible. She could see in the future for Arthur only hate and strife and power overthrown and life hunted by those who thirst for his blood, while you she knew though you might attain momentary greatness, could not and would not feel it's effects. Zamorna has cast her aside as revenge. She cannot hate him for an instant and she cannot bow to fate. She is sinking fast and cannot possibly sustain her agony long. If she could see Zamorna, if she could hear him speak, I believe she would rejoice to die! Your name she hardly mentions for she must know that her ruin is owning to you.

NORTHANGERLAND: (*Branwell*) She will not see him, he shall be defeated. I will not lose all that I have to Zamorna.

It is left up to Anne to keep the fiction alive.

ANNE: Some of the constitutionalists had still a lingering partiality for Zamorna, like that of an indulgent father for a prodigal son. But the wish prevailed throughout the city of annihilation for him and his. Tuesday told them it was granted, that the Angrian army was ruined, the Angrian nation freed and the Angrian King routed.

Enter Branwell as Northangerland and Charlotte as Zamorna with swords to do battle.

NORTHANGERLAND: (*Branwell*) Through the hoarse howlings of the storm I saw but did I truly see, A glimpse of that unearthly form, Whose name has once been Victory? 'Twas but a glimpse and all seems past, For cares like clouds again return, And I'll forget him, till the blast For ever from my soul has torn, That vision of a Mighty Man Crushed into Dust.

Branwell and Charlotte begin to fight, the fight goes on as background to the poem

EMILY: He sees his soldiers round him falling In vain to Heaven for Vengeance calling, He sees them lie, with glaring eye, Turned up toward him, that wandering star Who led them still from good to ill, In hopes of power to meet with war And fall from noontide dreams of glory To this strange rest, so grim and gory.

ANNE: When rolling on those friends o'erthrown, War's wildest wreck breaks thundering down Zamorna's pale and ghastly brow, Darkens with anguish – all in vain, To stem the tide of battle now, For every rood of that wide plain
Is heaped with thousands of his dead.

EMILY: 'Tis hopeless and he knows it so/

ANNE: /That eye! Oh I have seen it shine Mid scenes that differed far from these. I saw him in his beauty's pride With manhood on his brow, The falcon-eyed with heart of pride/

EMILY: /I knew him and I marked him then For one apart, as far, From the surrounding crowds of men As heaven's remotest star, I saw him in the battle's hour And conquered by his side.

ANNE: I was with him in his height of power, And triumph of his pride, 'Tis past but I am with him now, Where he spurs fiercely through the fight,

EMILY: I see them falling in the storm 'Mid crowds of horse, that wildly ride, Above each gashed and trampled form, His charger shot, Zamorna down, 'Mong foes and

66

friends alike o'erthrown.

ANNE: Yet never may that desperate soul, Betray the thoughts which o'er it roll, For everyone on earth might die And not a tear should strain that eye Or force a single sob or sigh, From him who cannot yield

EMILY: Yet stay one moment – 'tis but one, A single glance to heaven is thrown, One frenzied burst of grief – 'Tis gone His heart once more is steeled, That was a burst of anguish there Blazed all the intenseness of despair It said 'Oh all is lost forever.'

ANNE: All he loves to him is dead All his hopes of glory fled All the past is vanished Save what nought can sever Ever living memories, That shall haunt him till he die With things that he can realise

Charlotte is finally defeated but from a position of yielding on the ground raises her head to shout

ZAMORNA: (*Charlotte*) Never, never , never.

Emily and Anne carry her off.

NORTHANGERLAND:(*Branwell*) I said I saw his anguished glance Say did he think on me? Incendiary of rebel France Parrot of Liberty? The wretched traitor who let in, Of Afric's opened land, Deceit and craft and cant and sin, In one united band. Who raised the standard of Reform, And shouted 'Earth be free', To whelm his country in the storm Of rebel Tyranny, Who called himself the good right hand And father of the King, Only on his adopted land, This awful curse to bring. Yes, it was I and only , Who hurled Zamorna down, From conquering glory placed on high This day to be o'erthrown. I heft the sword to leave him dead, I pierced my Sovereign's breast, And only on my guilty head May all his sufferings rest.

It appears that Branwell is prepared to take full responsibility for his actions in defeating Charlotte. And their lives will never be the same.

BLACKOUT

ACT THREE SCENE ONE

The Four Brontes on stage.

EMILY: Come, the wind may never again blow as now it blows for us,

ANNE: And the stars may never again shine as now they shine.

BRANWELL: Long before October returns, Seas of blood will have parted us

CHARLOTTE: And you must crush the love in your heart, And I the love in mine.

ANNE: For face to face will our kindred stand,

EMILY: And as they are, so shall we be

ANNE: forgetting how the same sweet earth has bourne and nourished us all.

BRANWELL: One must fight for the people's power

CHARLOTTE: And one for the rights of the Royalty

EMILY: And each be ready to give his life to work the others fall.

ANNE: The change of war we cannot shun, Nor would we shrink from our fathers cause

BRANWELL: nor dread Death more because the hand that gives it may be near.

ANNE: We must bear to see ambition rule over love with his iron laws.

EMILY: Must yield our blood for a stranger's sake, and refuse ourselves a tear.

CHARLOTTE: So the wind may never again blow as now it blows for us

BRANWELL: And the stars may never again shine as now they shine.

CHARLOTTE: Next October the cannon's roar from hostile ranks may be urging us.

BRANWELL: Me to strike for your life's blood and you to strike for mine

BLACKOUT

Emily is onstage as Mary Percy. Duchess of Zamorna, Rogue's daughter and Duoro's wife.

ANNE: There is something peculiarly sad in the numbness of sensation that succeeds intense suffering. Mary, the Duchess of Zamorna could not feel for ever the biting and bitter pain that when separation was fresh, hunted her day and night. Days and weeks had now passed since the fall, the capture and punishment of Zamorna. It had been tenderly revealed to her that his ship, the Rover, was wrecked on the open Atlantic and that since that event no trace could be discovered, no tidings gained of the exile. The last three years of her life had become strangely visionary to her. The remembrances of a thousand characters who had moved and shone around her was grown dim and vague.

MARY:*(Emily)* I am maddening myself with the image. I wish it would leave me. It is very vivid. I cannot bear it because through all this winter, through all next spring, through all the lovely days of summer –through autumn and further, further still if I should live so long, I shall see him no more. He is dead. How shall I pass the night before me?

71

Emily mimes reading the letter in the foreground as Charlotte as Zamorna appears in the background.

ZAMORNA: (Charlotte) By this time you and all the world believe that I am dead. Robert has done me a good turn in spreading such a report but he knows well I was not on board the Rover when she was wrecked. For yourself, cherish life, I will win you back sometime. No sea rolls between us now – not so much as a river or a rill. I may be far nearer than you think. I have a task to perform before I see you but when that is accomplished I think there are few earthly obstacles that will keep me from you. You know to what commissioners Northangerland has deputed the government of the kingdom. I think I feel an impulse in the region of my heart which will enable me to give your father's Lieutenants some trouble. Colnemoss and Edwardston are still covered with corpses. I think when I have earned a right to bury them a certain suffering sensation I have in my breast will be a little relieved. I should like to have you in my arms for a moment but I suppose that is not to be as yet. If you are strong enough, come down to the park-gates tomorrow at nine o'clock in the morning and you will perhaps see me but don't expect to speak to me. I am not lurking about like a felon but following my calling in an independent way. I defy the devil himself either to catch or retain me just now.

There's a lock of my hair enclosed. You've romance enough about you to like the gift. This letter sounds rather hard and rough but I've had something to go through lately. I don't intend to die in a hurry. Goodbye.

MARY: *(Emily)* My father! Will he banish him again? I must go to Ellrington Hall where I can watch him. O God, look upon Zamorna, guard his life, give him victory, crush his foes and above all, in life or death, let him not forget me. *(reads)* Great movement in the East! Return of Zamorna! Battle of Ardsley! Defeat of the Allied Troops.

I could read with rapture but my father, that recollection brings agony. Oh what will he do? Treachery all around him, the Angrians, all wild fury, full of savage thirst for his blood. And they are advancing led by Zamorna – Zamorna the man he exiled, the soldier he fettered from action in the midst of his whirlwind career, the king he tore away from his darling country. But listen, my father comes. I will hide these papers. I dare not let him see them.

Enter Anne as Louisa Vernon

LOUISA: *(Anne)* It is over! It is over and we are victims crushed and bound. I see round us scaffolds. I feel the edge of the descending steel. I hear the blood streaming – oh- Rogue! But stay, who is this – like – hideously like- it must be – it is his daughter. You! You! I know you. Have

73

we not glorious news this morning. Your paramour is upon us. Now go sell your father – barter him at a price – so many months of Zamorna's love. He won't have you for his wife you know, but perhaps you may do for his mistress.

MARY:(*Emily*) What can she be? Is the person sane?

LOUISA: (*Anne*) What can I be? I am the woman who has had the power to fascinate Northangerland, to make him desert his wife and banish his friend, to make him revolutionise Africa. I am Lousia Vernon.

MARY: *(Emily)* I thought as much. I never saw you before. Till now you have been nothing more to me than an annoying word, a nuisance of sound. Now leave the room – this is my apartment – I do not wish to be troubled by you.

LOUISA: *(Anne)* Leave it? Miss Mary or whatever your name is, I would have you to understand I am not accustomed to such language in this house. It is my own. Am I not Lady Protectoress? Go! Or my servants shall carry you away. I will ring the bell.

Enter Branwell as Rogue (Northangerland)

LOUISA:*(Anne)* Oh Alexander, my Alexander. You will save me from every insult, you will save me from danger. Don't let me be guillotined. Look at my neck – you would not like it to be gashed with the sharp axe and they are coming – they will take me - they will behead me. Look he smiles!

74

Are you glad? Well it is all your own doing. You have brought them. You would not listen to me and slay whilst you had the power. I wanted you to kill and you only banished. Fool, it serves you right – he is come back. I wish he may take you and kill you

NORTHANGERLAND: *(Branwell)* Thank you my love. I need some good wishes and I'm likely to get them. Meantime, what has occasioned this burst of fondness? Any special news this morning?

LOUISA: (*Anne*) Zamorna has re-appeared in Angria, has taken the command of the Angrian forces and the East has risen from Olympia to Gazemba. Their whole cry is Verdopolis! Vengeance on republican Verdopolis and Oh Alexander – down with the Demagogue. Doom to the Usurper! Blood to him that has shed blood. How are you to be saved? The earth yawns on all sides. There is no bridge over the abyss. Must you slip, sink, vanish?

NORTHANGERLAND: *(Branwell)* Aye if that is my fate. All this is very much my own work and I am not more unhappy at this crisis than in hours of dead calm, so shed no tears for the matter and as for these Angrians, do as you will.

BLACKOUT

ACT THREE SCENE THREE

Anne, Charlotte and Emily on stage

ANNE: All the summer plains of Angria were asleep in perfect peace And the soldier as he rested deemed that foreign wars would cease All the slain were calmly buried – the survivors home returned, Crossed again the silent thresholds –where their faithful consorts mourned.

CHARLOTTE: And the knight, who never yielded, in the battle to a foe Now like Manoah's sun is fettered, with encircling arms of snow.

EMILY: And why may not soldiers rest, when the fiery charge is sped They may gather thorn-less flowers who on bristled spears have bled.

ANNE: Wherefore then that sound of trumpets sent at noonday through the land?

EMILY: Why that rustling waft of banners and that gathering band by band?

ANNE: Are there hosts upon the frontiers, are there ships upon the sea?

EMILY: Are there chains in senates forging, for the children of the free?

CHARLOTTE: No though every foe is conquered and though every field is won, Yet Zamorna thinks his labours for the Kingdom but begun.

ANNE: And those trumpets are his summons –those deep bugles are his call,

EMILY: From bower, to couch and chamber, he has raised his nobles all.

CHARLOTTE: The horse again is saddled, that from conflict scarce has breathed. The sabre flashed in daylight, that the peace had hardly sheathed.

EMILY: And vaulting to their chargers, a hundred heroes spring

ANNE: Yes ten thousand to Gazemba are gone to meet the King,

EMILY: Forth staff and plume and banner, forth crest and sword and lance,

ANNE: Amid the battery's thunder, the royal guards advance.

EMILY: A flash from every cannon – a shout from every man.

ANNE: For the King is dashing forward, he is spurring to the van.

CHARLOTTE: You have followed me in danger,

ANNE: Says the monarch to his men.

CHARLOTTE: When we scarce had hope to cheer us – will you follow me again? While you keep my kingdom free, I will reign your sovereign true While your hearts are staunch for me, shall my hand be strong for you.

ANNE: The trumpets breathed a thrill and then paused,

then wild and high Pipe and horn and clarion shrill, burst in triumph on the sky.

EMILY: With hearts too rapt for words, stood the troops as still as death Then arose a clash of swords but there never stirred a breath.

Enter Branwell with swords. He fights Charlotte but the fight ends with him throwing down his sword in disgust and walking out.

CHARLOTTE: (triumphant) Sound the loud trumpet, o'er Afric's bright sea Zamorna has triumphed, the Angrians are free. Sing for the sun has arisen on Creation, Sound ye the Trumpet to herald his dawn Rise man and Monarch and City and Nation, Away with your midnight and Hail to your morn, Sound the Loud Trumpet o'er land and o'er sea Join Hearts and Voices rejoicing to sing, Africa arising hath sworn to be free, And Glory to Angria and God Save our King.

Exit Emily and Anne. Charlotte sits down to write a letter.

CHARLOTTE: (writing) Branwell has been conducting himself very badly lately.

BLACKOUT

78

ACT THREE SCENE FOUR

Charlotte and Branwell sit on the floor together as of old, constructing a story. They will act out the narrations given from their writing slopes by Emily and Anne.

EMILY: The course of things in this world is strange, inscrutable. Mary died and for seventeen years her husband Douro gave himself up to the wildest extravagances of vice. During those seventeen years he never spoke of Mary Percy – never revived by words the remembrance of her features, her voice, her pure life and saintly death. At last we see him again spent almost with sin – lying down looking upwards, confiding his long pent-up feelings to an ear which to us seems all unmeet for the Confession.

ANNE: Who can calculate the probabilities or possibilities of this our changeful life? Percy, who had never referred to his daughter or her actions or his feelings towards her since the first spadeful of earth run hollow upon his coffin-lid, now contradicts every habit of his life and befriends Douro.

EMILY: Douro pestered him – thwarted him - opposed his will, counteracted his projects, ridiculed his peculiarities, stormed at his prejudices – and still he endured.

ANNE: True Ellrington broke upon his young comrade

79

sometimes with fury, and at other times he seemed to freeze and turn away with hollow coolness from him. But Douro could meet Percy's passion with wilder passion and it so happened that Rogue, even when intoxicated, never inflicted on him the reckless violence by which he had certainly shortened the life of some of his own associates.

EMILY: Once or twice he is known to have held his sword to Douro's breast, after some mad provocation of the young scoundrel, but he never ran him through, though dared to do it by the bold tongue and defying eyes of his prostrate vice-president.

ANNE: Yet after all, twenty four hours would hardly elapse before they would be bound together again, perhaps reasoning calmly on things high and sublime like Milton's Angels – perhaps sitting almost silently side by side – or it may be again in the furious contention –ready to drink each other's hearts blood.

Exit Charlotte. Branwell, as Northangerland comes across to Emily. He looks through her papers, beseeching her...

NORTHANGERLAND: (*Branwell*) Is Arthur here?

EMILY: No

NORTHANGERLAND (*Branwell*) Where is he Zenobia?

EMILY: I don't know. Last time I saw him he was talking to the Duchess in Lady Helen's drawing room – but that was just after tea.

Branwell goes up to Charlotte, now seated at her own writing slope – ignoring him.

NORTHANGERLAND:(*Branwell)* Is Arthur here?

CHARLOTTE: No

NORTHANGERLAND: *(Branwell)* Where is he mother?

CHARLOTTE: I don't know my son – what do you want with him?

BRANWELL: I only want to tell him he has been long enough here. I can't bear his commotion, he keeps the house in too great a bustle. Damn him!

Charlotte puts down her writing slope and dressed up as Douro. She comes to the couch, where Branwell is lying, alone and dejected. There is an uncomfortable confusion about whether they are both in character or not.

CHARLOTTE: Hey, all darkness!

BRANWELL: I desire you won't ring for candles.

CHARLOTTE: What are you doing here by yourself? Come now, you're no worse this evening are you?

BRANWELL: I'm worse every evening.

CHARLOTTE: On the contrary, I believe you improve daily. I could not help noticing to Zenobia this morning how bucking you were beginning to look in the silks and smalls.

BRANWELL: Your language is unpleasant to me and there's a kind of jaunty slang in all you say which annoys me extremely.

CHARLOTTE: Oh you get so refined and romantic with living out of the world. I think now if I could get you off to a fashionable watering place – Mowbray for instance – it would do you an incredible deal of good.

BRANWELL: (*rising to leave but pinned down by Douro*) Have you entered into a conspiracy to send me to Mowbray?

CHARLOTTE: I don't know. I'm thinking about it, especially if you don't shake off these solitary habits.

BRANWELL: Damn you, none of your hectoring.

CHARLOTTE: Now what new crotchet has come over you? Why you remind me of nobody so much as Louisa Vernon – you've all her ladyship's theatrical starts and trances and capricious changes of temper.

BRANWELL: Where is Lousia now? Is she still in your custody?

CHARLOTTE: Yes, safe enough, I keep her at a little place on the other side of Calabar.

BRANWELL: Do you ever see her?

CHARLOTTE: I saw her once about three weeks since, for the first time since my return from the Cirhala.

BRANWELL: Are you sure it was the first time?

CHARLOTTE: Yes sir, why do you ask me so particularly – surely you're not jealous you old Puritan.

BRANWELL: I never had occasion to be jealous of you yet, but Louisa is very pretty.

CHARLOTTE: Never fear Sir, I think your tastes and mine are very much opposed. I never thought Vernon pretty – she's so dark and fierce.

BRANWELL: Does she frighten you then... Arthur?

CHARLOTTE: Sometimes, especially when she turns sentimental.

BRANWELL: then the witch tries that method with you now and then. Now confess the truth, has she not made love to you sometimes.

CHARLOTTE: Very furiously (laughs)

BRANWELL: Damn her! What did she say?

CHARLOTTE: That she adored me. Then she jumped up, threw her arms around me and kissed me to her hearts content.

BRANWELL: What did you do?

CHARLOTTE: Why, what would you have done under the circumstances?

BRANWELL: Surrendered at discretion to be sure.

CHARLOTTE: But I did not *(walks over to where Anne as Louisa has entered)* I begged her to be more composed –but that was out of the question.

83

LOUSIA: (*Anne*) People say you are wild! But I am sure you are not – I never saw anything like gallantry about you yet. You seem to be impenetrable to love, neither music, mirth, sentiment, vivacity nor even an absolute declaration of intense passion can make the least impression on you. Even as you smile at me just now, there is something so scornful about your lips. I do hate you! I abhor you! I could kill you. But still, still, I love you too till my heart aches as if it would break.

Charlotte crosses back to Branwell at the couch.

CHARLOTTE: *(as Douro)*Now sire, what do you think of that?

Exit Charlotte and Anne crosses to Branwell.

LOUISA: *(Anne)*   Will   you   come   to   supper?
NORTHANGERLAND:(*Branwell*) They have left me.

Re-enter Charlotte – showing him a piece of paper

CHARLOTTE: Do you remember this?

He nods, reading from the paper

84

CHARLOTTE: What are your sisters names?

BRANWELL: Charlotte Wiggins, Jane Wiggins and Anne Wiggins.

CHARLOTTE: Are they as queer as you?

BRANWELL: Oh they are miserable silly creatures not worth talking about. Charlotte, eighteen years old, a broad dumpy thing, whose head does not come higher than my elbows, Emily's sixteen, lean and scant with a face about the size of a penny, and Anne is nothing, absolutely nothing.

CHARLOTTE: What is she an idiot?

BRANWELL: Next to it.

Exit Charlotte. Branwell sits and writes on the other side of the paper reading it out loud as he does so.

BRANWELL: I grew weary of heroics and longed for some chat with men of common clay.

BLACKOUT

ACT THREE SCENE FIVE

Enter Charlotte and sits at the table to write.

CHARLOTTE: I have now written a great many books and for a long time dwelt on the same characters and scenes and subjects. But we must change, for the eye is tired of the picture so oft recurring and now so familiar. Yet, it is no easy theme to dismiss from my imagination the images which have filled it so long, they were my friends and intimate acquaintances, they peopled my thoughts by day and not seldom stole strangely even into my dreams by night. Charlotte Bronte July 1839.

Exit Charlotte. Enter Emily sits down to write.

EMILY: A paper to be opened when Anne is twenty five years old, or my next birthday after, if all be well. Emily Jane Bronte. July the 30th 1841. It is Friday evening near nine o'clock –wild rainy weather. I am seated in the dining room alone writing this document .

Enter Anne sits on the couch to write

ANNE: Scarborough July the 30th A.D. 1841. This is Emily's birthday. She has now completed her twenty third year and is, I believe, at home.

EMILY: The Gondalians are at present in a threatening state, but there is no open rupture as yet. All the princes and princesses of the Royalty are at the palace of Instruction.

ANNE: How will it be when we open this paper and the one Emily has written in four years time? I wonder whether the Gondalians will still be flourishing and what will be their condition?

EMILY: And now I must close, sending from far an exhortation 'courage, courage' to exiled and harassed Anne, wishing she was here.

ANNE: We are now all separate, and not likely to meet for many a weary week.

Exit Emily and Anne. Enter Branwell, sits down to write.

BRANWELL: Haworth August 4th 1845. Dear Sir. John Brown wishes to know whether or not you can make your intended visit to Haworth this week. I need hardly add that I shall myself be most delighted to see you, as God knows I have a tolerably heavy load on my mind just now and would look to an hour spent with one like yourself as a means of at least temporarily lightening it. I returned yesterday from a week's journey to Liverpool and North Wales but I found during my absence that wherever I went a certain woman, robed in black, and calling herself 'misery' walked by my side and leant on my arm as affectionately as if she were my legal wife. Like some other husbands I could have spared her presence. Yours most sincerely, Patrick Branwell Bronte.

BLACKOUT

ACT THREE SCENE SIX

Emily and Anne sit writing.

EMILY: Haworth Tuesday July 30th 1845. My birthday. Showery, breezy, cool. I am twenty seven years old today.

ANNE: We have had so far a very cold, wet summer.

EMILY: The Gondals still flourish bright as ever.

ANNE: We have not yet finished our Gondal Chronicles that we began three years and a half ago. Emily is writing some poetry too, I wonder what it is about?

EMILY: I must hurry off to my turning and ironing.

Exit Emily. Enter Charlotte and looks over the papers that Emily has left.

CHARLOTTE: One day in the autumn of 1845 I accidentally lighted upon a manuscript volume of verse in my sister Emily's handwriting. Of course I was not surprised, knowing that she could and did write verse; I looked it over and something more than surprise seized me – a deep conviction that these were not common effusions, nor at all like the poetry women generally write. I thought them condensed and terse, vigorous and genuine. To my ear they had also a peculiar music, wild , melancholy and elevating.

She reads a poem – as she does so Emily re-enters and stands shocked to hear Charlotte read her work.

CHARLOTTE: Lord of Elbe on Elbe Hill The mist is thick and the wind is chill, And the heart of thee freed from the dawn of day, Has sighed for sorrow that thou went away.
Bright are the fires in thy lonely home, I see them far off and as deepens the gloom. Gleaming like stars through the high forest –boughs, Gladder they glow in the park's repose O Alexander! When I return, Warm as those hearths my heart would burn. Light as thine own my foot would fall,
If I might hear they voice in the hall. But thou art now on a desolate sea, Parted from Gondal and parted from me. All my repining is hopeless and vain, Death never yields back his victims again.

Emily wrests the volume from Charlotte

EMILY: None but one beheld him dying, Parting with the parting day, Winds of evening sadly sighing Bore his soul from earth away.

Anne comments on the awkward stand off between Charlotte and Emily.

ANNE: Emily was not a person of demonstrative character,

nor one on whom the recesses of whose mind and feelings even those nearest and dearest to her could, with impugnity, intrude unlicenced.

CHARLOTTE: It took hours to reconcile her to the discovery I had made. But as we read through the poems another world came to light, the secret world of Gondal known hitherto only to Emily and Anne.

Emily now plays Augusta and Branwell enters to play Alexander.

AUGUSTA(Emily) O wander not so far away, O love forgive this selfish tear. It may be sad for thee to stay, But how can I live lonely here?

ANNE: Augusta sat watching by that water side, The light of life expiring slow from his fair cheek. There he lay among the bloom, His red blood dyed a deeper hue.. Shuddering to feel the ghostly gloom, That coming Death around him threw. Sickening to think one hour would sever, The sweet, sweet world and him for ever. Maddening with despair and pride, He turned his dying face to her and wildly cried/

ALEXANDER: (*Branwell*) /Oh once again, Might I my native country see! But once again – one single day! And must it – can it never be? To die, and die so far away When life has hardly smiled for me. Augusta – you will

91

soon return, Back to that land in health and bloom. And then the heath alone will mourn above my unremembered tomb. For you'll forget the lonely grave, And mouldering corpse by Elinor's wave.

Branwell as Alexander dies and Emily as Augusta is carried off by Charlotte and Anne as if under arrest.

BLACKOUT

ACT THREE SCENE SEVEN

Charlotte on stage with Emily lying on the couch as Augusta.

CHARLOTTE: (reading) O God of heaven! The dream of horror, The frightful dream is over now. The sickened heart, the blasting sorrow, The ghastly night, the ghastlier morrow. The aching sense of utter woe. The burning tears that would keep welling, The groans that mocked at every tear. That burst from out their dreary dwelling, As if each gasp were life expelling, But life was nourished by despair

AUGUSTA:*(Emily)* It's over now and I am free. And the ocean wind is caressing me The wild wind from that wavy main I never thought to see again. My voice is choked but not with grief, And salt drops from my haggard cheek Descend like rain upon the heath. How long they've wet a dungeon floor Falling on flag-stones damp and grey. I used to weep even in my sleep. The night was dreadful, like the day.

ANNE: But this is past and why return o'er such a past to brood and mourn. Shake off the fetters, break the chain And live and love and smile again The waste of youth, the waste of years departed in that dungeon's thrall. The gnawing grief, the hopeless tears, Forget them, O forget them all.

Enter Branwell. He stands and watches his sisters.

CHARLOTTE: (reading) King Julius left the south country, His banners all bravely flying

ANNE: His followers went out with Jubilee but they shall return with sighing.

CHARLOTTE: Loud arose the triumphal hymn, The drums were loudly rolling

ANNE: Yet you might have heard in distance dim how a passing bell was tolling

EMILY: (stands) The sword so bright from battles won with unseen rust is fretting.

CHARLOTTE: That evening comes before the noon, The scarce risen sun is setting

ANNE: While princes hang upon his breath, And nations round are fearing

EMILY: Close by his side a daggered death With sheathless point stands sneering

Charlotte stabs Branwell and he falls to the ground.

CHARLOTTE: That death he took a certain aim,

ANNE: For death is stony-hearted

CHARLOTTE: And in the zenith of his fame, Both power and life departed.

Emily turns away and again dresses in Augusta's cloak.

AUGUSTA: *(Emily)* When will he come? Twill soon be night
He'll come when evening falls
CHARLOTTE: Lady; Brenzaida's crest is down Brenzaida's
sun is set Lady, His empires overthrown!

Charlotte forces Emily/Augusta to look at the fallen Branwell.

ANNE: He died beneath his palace dome True hearts on
every side
CHARLOTTE: I saw him fall, I saw the gore, From his
heart's fountain swell

Tired of the taunting, Emily knocks Charlotte down. It should be a sharp, shocking move – and very real!

EMILY: And mingling on the marble floor His murderer's
life-blood fell, For who forgives the accursed crime Of
dastard treachery. Rebelling in its chosen time May
freedom's champion be. Revenge may stain a righteous
sword, It may be just to slay, But traitor, traitor – from
that word All true breasts shrink away!

Emily and Anne exit carrying Branwell, leaving Charlotte on her own centre stage.

CHARLOTTE: So foes pursue, and cold allies Mistrust me every one. Let me be false in others eyes If faithful in my own.

BLACKOUT

ACT THREE SCENE EIGHT

Emily, Branwell and Anne are sitting together onstage. Enter Charlotte.

CHARLOTTE: Were they shepherds, who sat all day, on that brown mountainside? But neither staff nor dog they had, Nor woolly flock to guide. They were clothed in savage attire, Their locks were dark and long. And at each belt a weapon dire, Like bandit knife was hung. One was a woman tall and fair, A princess she might be. From her stately form, and her features rare and her look of majesty. 'Twas well she had no sceptre to wield, no subject land to sway.Fear might have made her vassals yield but Love had been far away.

ANNE: Yet Love was even at her feet In his most burning mood.

CHARLOTTE: That love which will the wicked greet as kindly as the good.

Emily and Branwell ignore Charlotte, shutting her out of their world.

BRANWELL: (to Emily) Augusta, from my very birth I have been nursed in strife, And lived upon this weary Earth a wanderer all my life. The baited tiger could not be so much

97

athirst for gore, For men and laws have tortured me, Till I can bear no more.

EMILY: The guiltless blood upon my hands Will shut me out from Heaven. And here, and even in foreign lands I cannot find a haven.

BRANWELL:(*turns to Charlotte*) For thee, through never-ending years I'd suffer endless pain. But only give me back my tears, Return my love again.

CHARLOTTE: I've known a hundred kinds of love, All made the loved one rue, And what is thine that it should prove Than other love more true?

BRANWELL: Listen, I've known a burning heart To which my own was given, Nay, not in passion, do not start, Our love was love from heaven. My soul dwelt with her day and night She was my all sufficing light. My childhood's mate, my boyhood's guide, My only blessing, only pride.

Emily senses she is losing Branwell from her 'world.' She cannot forgive Charlotte even if he can.

EMILY: But cursed be that very earth, That gave that fiend her fatal birth! With her own hand she bent the bow, That laid my best affections low.

Her words pull Branwell up short.

BRANWELL: And mocked my grief and scorned my prayers And drowned my bloom of youth in tears. Warnings, reproaches, both were vain – What recked she of another's pain?

ANNE and EMILY: We both were scorned – both sternly driven To shelter 'neath a foreign heaven.

Chickens are coming home to roost. Charlotte will not yield to the pressure.

CHARLOTTE: I will not now those days recall, The oath within that cavernous hall and it's fulfilment, those you know. We both together struck the blow.

EMILY: But you can never know the pain, That my lost heart did then sustain. When severed wide by guiltless gore I felt that one could love no more.

They all now act out the parts described in the dialogue. Emily is the 'enemy.'

CHARLOTTE: Now hear me in these regions wile I saw today my enemy, Unarmed, as helpless as a child she slumbered on a sunny lee.Two friends, no other guard had she. My hand was raised, my knife was bare, With stealthy tread I stole along. But a wild bird sprang from his hidden lair, And woke her with a sudden song.

Charlotte is standing over Emily poised to kill her.

CHARLOTTE: Yet moved she not, she only raised her lids and on the bright sun gazed. And uttered such a dreary sigh, I thought just then she should not die, Since living was such misery. Assist me with my heart and hand - To send to hell my mortal foe.

Charlotte stabs Emily, Branwell and Anne rush towards her.

CHARLOTTE: In vain in vain you need not gaze upon those features now. That sinking head you need not raise Nor kiss that pulseless brow

Branwell cradles Emily in his arms, Charlotte stabs him too.

ANNE: *(to Branwell)* Let out the grief that chokes your heart Lord Lesley, set it free, The sternest eye, for such a death might fill with sympathy.
BRANWELL: Her heart is beating. She is not really gone Oh death delay, Thy last fell dart to throw. Till I can hear my Sovereign say The traitor's heads are low. God guard her life, since not to me that dearest boon was given. God bless her arm with victory Or bless me not with heaven.
ANNE: Then came the cry of agony, The pang of parting

pain, And he had overpassed the sea that none can pass again.

Emily gets up and goes towards Charlotte.

EMILY: Oh I have wrongs to pay. Give life, give vigour now.

We fear more physical violence.

ANNE: She turns, she meets the Murderer's gaze. Her own is scorched with sudden blaze.

Emily throws Charlotte a sword and they fight. Both are wounded by Charlotte wins.

ANNE: The blood streams down her brow. The blood streams through her coal black hair. She strikes it off with little care, She scarcely feels it flow. For she has marked and known him too And her own heart's ensanguined dew Must slake her vengeance now.

As Emily falls to the ground defeated she shouts

EMILY: False friend
ANNE: (*to Charlotte*)No tongue save thine can tell the mortal strife that then befell.

CHARLOTTE: Ere the night darkened down The stream in silence sang once more. And on its green bank, bathed in gore Augusta lay alone.

Exit Charlotte. Branwell gets up and rushes across to where Emily lies.

BRANWELL: Long he gazed and held his breath, Kneeling on the bloodstained heat. Long he gazed those lids beneath Looking into death.

Anne goes across to join him.

BRANWELL: Not a word from his followers fell. They stood by mute and pale. That black treason uttered well its own heart harrowing tale.
ANNE: But earth was bathed in other gore. There were crimson drops across the moor, And Lord Eldred glancing round, Saw those tokens on the ground.

BRANWELL: Bring him back. Wounded is the traitor fled. Vengeance may hold but minutes brief, And you have all your lives for grief.

Anne goes off in search of Charlotte and Branwell carries Emily to the couch, set as it was in the opening scene. Emily speaks to Branwell from the couch.

EMILY: And thou art gone, with all thy pride Thou so adored, so deified.

Exit Branwell. Enter Anne, crosses to Emily and places her hand on Emily's head.

ANNE: Cold as the earth unweeting now, Of love, or joy, or mortal woe.

Exit Emily. Anne sits down on the couch. Enter Charlotte

CHARLOTTE: For what thou wert I would not grieve, But much for what thou wert to be.

Exit Anne

CHARLOTTE: And vain too must the sorrow be of those who live to mourn for thee. But Gondal's foes shall not complain That thy dear blood was poured in vain.

BLACKOUT

ACT THREE SCENE NINE

CHARLOTTE: (writing) It took hours to reconcile her to the discovery I had made, and days to persuade her that such poems merited publication. I knew, however, that a mind like hers could not be without some latent spark of honourable ambition and refused to be discouraged in my attempts to fan that spark to flame. We agreed to arrange a small selection of our poems.

Enter Branwell

BRANWELL: Patrick Branwell Bronte died of consumption, brought on by a chill he caught one night returning from the Black Bull Public House on 24th September 1848 at the age of Thirty One.

Enter Emily

EMILY: Emily Jane Bronte caught a chill at Branwell's funeral. She never left the house from that date and died of consumption on 19th December 1848 aged thirty. She had published one novel, Wuthering Heights before her death. It shocked contemporary critics.

Enter Anne

ANNE: Despite going to Scarborough in an attempt to hold her consumption at bay, Anne Bronte died there on 28th May 1849 aged twenty nine. She had published two novels before her death.

CHARLOTTE: Charlotte Bronte lived to see three novels published before her death, following complications during pregnancy, on 31st March 1855 aged thirty nine.

The four join together

CHARLOTTE: We wove a web in childhood A web of sunny air,

ANNE: We dug a spring in infancy, Of water pure and fair

EMILY: We sowed in youth a mustard seed, We cut an almond rod

CHARLOTTE: We are grown up to a riper age, Are they withered in the sod?

ANNE: Are they blighted, failed and faded, Are they mouldered back to clay?

BRANWELL: For life is darkly shaded, And it's joys fleet fast away

ANNE: Faded! The web is still of air, But how its folds are spread.

BRANWELL: And from its tints of crimson clear, How deep a glow is shed. The light of an Italian sky, Where clouds of sunset lingering lie Is not more ruby red.

EMILY: But the spring was under a mossy stone, Its jet may gush no more

CHARLOTTE: Hark! Sceptic bid thy doubts be done. Is that a feeble roar Rushing around thee?

BRANWELL: Lo the tide of waves where armed fleets may ride, Sinking and swelling, frowns and smiles, An ocean with a thousand isles

EMILY: And scarce a glimpse of shore.

BRANWELL: Dream that stole o'er us in the time, When life was in its vernal clime

EMILY: Dream that still faster o'er us steals, As the mild star of spring declining, The advent of that day reveals That glows on Sirius' fiery shining

ANNE: Oh! As thou swellest and as the scenes, Cover this cold word's darkest features

CHARLOTTE: Stronger each change my spirit weans

ALL: To bow before thy god-like creatures.

BLACKOUT

CURTAIN

FURTHER READING:

I would recommend any (and all) of the following for those interested in finding out more about the Brontës.

Christine Alexander

2001-2005: (ed) Tales of the Islanders by Charlotte Brontë– in 4 Volumes.

2003: The Oxford Companion to the Brontës.

1995: Branwell's Blackwood's Magazine, 1995

1995: Charlotte Brontë's High Life In Verdopolis.

1991: An Edition of The Early Writings of Charlotte Brontë: Volume II, Part 1 and Part 2: The Rise of Angria 1833-1835

1987: An Edition of The Early Writings of Charlotte Brontë,

1983:The Early Writings of Charlotte Brontë.

Juliet Barker:

2010: The Brontës. Published in US as The Brontës: Wild Genius on the Moors: The Story of a Literary Family.
1997: The Brontës, A Life in Letters.

For anyone interested in viewing rehearsal tapes of the original production a DVD is available from the publishers. Contact aytonpublishing@gmail.com

Cally Phillips - A Life in Stages:

My first theatrical experience was perhaps the most important one and according to recent internet research, occurred in February 1970, which means I had just turned seven, though I could have sworn it was a year or two before that. Anyway, through a range of 'interesting' circumstances I attended a dress rehearsal of *The Admirable Crichton* (by J.M.Barrie) at the Dundee Rep. There was a lot of shouting by the director. I think he was shouting at my mum (who was doing costumes) for the inappropriateness of bringing small children into the rehearsal. Allegedly, I was upset and in order to pacify me I was taken backstage to meet 'Crichton' (Google tells me he was played by Michael Stroud) after the rehearsal – to prove to me it was only 'acting.' It was not so much the smell of the grease paint that got me hooked as the whole backstage environment.

My mum worked in costume at the Rep for a while and I have other backstage memories of playing around the costume store. Reflecting now, some forty years on, I realise that the role the theatre has played in my life has always been one at least equally about the 'behind the scenes' activity and magic as it has been about the onstage performance.

Twenty years after that first theatrical encounter, I wrote my first play. It was another stage in the journey I'm writing about here, which is essentially a retrospective of my dramatic 'life.'

What follows won't be strictly chronological because one thing I've found out in life (as in the theatre) is that while there is a beginning, middle and end structure to drama, they do not always fit into an easy, progressive narrative. As in my plays, *my* dramatic journey has beginnings and ends all over the place. My belief that 'the destination is in the journey' is perhaps nowhere expressed more clearly than in my stage work

BEGINNING

Apprenticeship (1980's) From usherette to leading lady.

When I arrived in London in 1984 armed with a degree in Moral Philosophy and a belief that the streets were paved with the route to fame and fortune, I was quickly disabused. During a hellish time working in sales, the theatre became my sanctuary. In fact I more or less lived in the National Theatre from the mid 80's to the mid 90's. When I wasn't selling, I was in a theatre in one capacity or another and I now look back on this as quite some apprenticeship. I can't begin to count the number of productions I saw but I was there in the heyday of Ian

McKellern at the National, Anthony Hopkins at the Old Vic and experienced Richard Harris playing Pirandello's Henry IV; which remains the stand out best piece of theatre I've ever seen, amidst a stellar line-up of plays. I bought playscripts and watched plays and lived and breathed high quality theatre on a weekly if not a daily basis.

You couldn't keep me out of the theatre. My backstage experience moved front of house. I became an usherette at the Secombe Centre Theatre in Sutton where I wielded a torch, a tray of ice creams, and tried to flog programmes. The lure of the greasepaint was strong and I joined Sutton Theatre Company, an amateur dramatics musical group with whom I performed for several shows. Musical theatre isn't really about acting though. And (for me) am dram really never 'cut it'. Too much about other things than the craft of acting. Too social and not serious enough. I won't deny it can be fun though.

In 1987 I performed in a semi-professional production of *Educating Rita* the Epsom Playhouse, taking the title role. After that it was front of house again as I earned the money to pay for a postrgraduate year at drama school by working at the Noel Coward Wine Bar in the Phoenix Theatre and subsequently at the Strand Theatre (now the Novello Theatre) where I ran the upper circle bar.

I found I loved working front of house in the theatre. Had I not had my sights set on the stage, I might well have gone into theatre or cinema administration. (Had the opportunity arisen I think I could have enjoyed that life – even in London.) I was paid £3 an hour and the sad fact was that it just didn't pay enough to live on – not when you did it five nights a week and all day on Saturdays. Not even if you worked full time, really.

However, the Noel Coward wine bar was FUN. And I learned a lot about wine (and about people who drink it in intervals.) I also learned how to add up very quickly and accurately in my head not only for giving change (tills didn't do that for you in those days) but for totting up at the end of the night. I couldn't go home (or more often go to a free late screening of a film – projectionists were great at getting you freebies!) until I'd got the figures to add up. That was some incentive.

The Phoenix was a great time. I liked the company, I liked the uniform (though I refused to wear a bow tie) and I liked the access to the theatre both front of house and backstage. I rubbed shoulders with many famous actors but it was in a working environment and I grew out of being star struck very early on. Even famous people can be moody and I have a (private) list of 'big names' and how pleasant they are as 'real' people outside their celebrity status. Too long to go into here sadly!

I left the Phoenix when I went to drama school in 1988 but I started at the Strand soon after because they had Sunday shows. I really needed the money by this stage (drama school is expensive!) and at my interview I both lied (saying I had experience of pulling pints which I didn't) and fainted. I was sitting on a bar stool and just keeled over backwards. I did things like that in those days – lack of food and high stress. I hit the ground, bounced back up and acted like nothing had happened (the drama school was teaching me something then!) and got the job. This time I had to wear a bow tie, but I got a winged collar shirt so I had to live with it. Needs must and all that.

Drama school had been a goal of mine for years. Be careful what you wish for! I got a place on the Post Graduate course at the Academy of Live and Recorded Arts, a place where they focussed on Stanislavskian technique (which was what I was interested in) as well as being strong in TV and Radio acting. I learned a lot there. Including that I really wasn't cut out to be an actress. Firstly, I could never work out what to do with my hands. Secondly, I could see that as a 'type' I wasn't that special and I would always be competing with others of my 'type' who had more going for them and/or better connections. But more importantly I couldn't hack the idea of a life spent waiting to be allowed to work.

So I left drama school before the final agent's shows, choosing, instead of being nameless girl in yet another drama school production of *The Children's Hour* to take the lead in a YMCA youth theatre production of *Gregory's Girl* where I played Dorothy. It combined theatre with another of my great loves – football. After the run I retired from acting.

Although I didn't know it then, the stage was now set for me to become a playwright. I didn't want to be a 'resting' actor. I wanted to work. I remember standing in line for benefits some months after I'd left drama school,then turned on my heel and walked out, deciding that I would never take benefits again – whatever I had to do I would earn my own living without having to rely on the state. It was an important decision. I don't regret it at all though it's meant some very tough times along the way. I determined to make a living out of my creativity. And I'm happy to say I've mostly achieved that. In the short term, I went back to sales repping – I still had to earn a living.

We Wove a Web in Childhood -research to writing (1989).

After another painful six months or so in sales, earning some big money, in 1990 I made a brave decision. I 'stopped the world' and got off. I went to live in Sheffield where I spent a lot of time in the library (never a hardship) researching what became my first play *We Wove A Web in Childhood.* It was a great time in many ways – I was working on my first computer – an Amstrad. Of course I

113

backed everything up onto big floppy discs. But that wasn't a lot of use when the computer and discs were stolen in a break in and I had to go back to scratch.

Unfortunately, all the copious research notes I'd made were lost in this theft. Fortunately, I'd got to the stage where I was ready to write the play and so I just had to 'go for it' using memory and what written notes I had. I imagine, being me, I still had plenty of them. I still do for anything I write. Even though I use the computer like an extension of my arm, I plan and structure on paper and I have a 'playbook' for each play. I started this when I became 'serious' about playwriting in the late 1990's. It was a habit I stole from my screenwriting career.

But in the spring and summer of 1990 I was hard at it writing my first play. Now I look back and think how interesting it is that I didn't have the confidence to actually write my own dialogue – the play is substantially an editing job since it uses exclusively the actual juvenilia and poems of the Brontes. What I brought to the party was dramatic structure and the underlying dramatic story. Through painstaking research I had worked out a chronological path through the mountains of tiny handwritten juvenilia (spending time at the Bronte Parsonage Museum Library whenever I could afford to get there and poring through the Shakespeare Head versions of the 'letters' and 'unpublished' work when I couldn't.) These days there's a lot more published Bronte juvenilia and several really good biographical works to aid such research, but for me it was hard on the eyes and hard on the brain trying to work out 'patterns'. It paid off though, as I still believe I came up with something uniquely interesting in drawing parallels between the writing and the 'real' lives.

Once the play was written, I got a job in London teaching English and Drama. During the following three years I was busy enough teaching not to take it too hard when the play got turned down everywhere I sent it. Nice comments most of the time, but the general opinion was that it was 'unproducable.' I guess it takes quite some leap of the imagination to believe that you can recreate the Battle of Waterloo on stage with four actors, but the end result of the comment 'it's unproducable' was simply for me to put my money and my time where my mouth was and decide to do it myself. This has become a pattern in my theatrical life. They tell you you can't do it. You do it anyway. It works. At least it's worked for me.

We Wove a Web in Childhood - the production 1993.

This was what was known as 'profit share' (though everyone understands that profit is a theoretical concept in this context!) I was directing as well as producing (I took on all these roles not out of megalomania but simply to keep costs down. It was the only way I knew I could get the play on. Necessity was the mother of invention. I ran auditions and held a six week rehearsal period. During which time I went through about three Charlotte's as they kept getting paid work. Finally I managed to get a great Charlotte, but she had to take a couple of days off during the run to complete a BBC drama – so I promised to understudy her part for those performances. That was me out of retirement, reluctantly I may say. But you know – the show must go on and all that.

Rehearsals are fun. I think that's part of the problem for actors and directors. It's really easy to lose sight of the fact that you are eventually going to perform for an audience and all too easy just to enjoy yourself in rehearsal.

That's why, subsequently, I've never run a long rehearsal period. I like actors to come prepared and then to work hard and fast, and I find that in two to three days you can get a rehearsed reading up and 'playing' and in a week or a fortnight at the most you can mount a really convincing production. You *can* do this if your writing is tight (by which I mean the dialogue is good enough for an actor to remember easily). I pride myself on writing dialogue that is both convincing to an audience and 'easy' for an actor. That's because I'm a trained actor and I know a) how to learn lines fast and b) how you use words structurally in a play.

Dialogue works on a number of levels. It has to sound realistic, sure, but it has to be constructed too. An interesting side point is reading dialogue off the page is quite a different experience to 'seeing' dialogue on stage. Many aspiring playwrights (and many theatre 'readers') don't fully appreciate this. But it's key. Poor dialogue really shows up on stage. Good dialogue can make the audience forget that the actor is in a black box, the wrong age, the wrong sex and even if they're holding a script, if the actor and the writing are good enough, you can get audiences to suspend disbelief. There are tricks to hide poor dialogue, sure. One of these is high production values, which means lavish set and costumes and all sorts of distractions which makes the audience buy into the event but to my mind, good dramatic writing is when you strip all that out and can still make an audience believe. That's always been my goal and I generally feel proud that I've achieved it as I intended in my produced stage work.

Benito Boccanegra, Come Back Molly Maguire (1990's).

Of course the stage is no more paved with gold than the streets and simply having a critical success and financially ruinous disaster with *We Wove A Web* (as with most theatre!) did not guarantee me any further success. I spent another two years in London and theatrically nothing happened. Instead, I turned most of my effort to screenwriting as a way to earn money from writing and I managed to do that for a good 10 years. I knew there was no money in the theatre. Not for me, anyway. But it didn't stop me writing plays when the thought occurred to me.

Benito Boccanegra's Big Break came to me when (for reasons too long to go into) I found myself trapped at the Royal Opera House in a performance of *Simone Boccanegra*. I don't like opera. It's a personal thing. I have reservations based on the fact that vibrato actually hurts my ears. Also, the amount of money spent on the productions pains me. Especially since I think they generally they make the acting in am dram musical theatre look acceptable! I love the plushness of the ROH of course and the backstage intrigues me as it does in any of these opulent traditional theatres, but the content – not for me.

So, to keep myself amused while enduring the performance I started writing an absurdist play (in the vein of *Rosencrantz and Guildenstern are Dead* mixed with *The Resistible Rise of Arturo Ui*) in my head. That combination of styles is, for me, fascinating. And my thoughts became the short play (as yet unperformed) *Benito Boccanegra's Big Break*.

In the years I've spent teaching playwriting, time and again I come across people who write scenes that are far

118

too short. With too many characters. *Benito Boccanegra* runs for 40 minutes maximum and it has some twenty scenes and a huge cast list (it runs through four time frames so the characters do double up). It is pretty much everything I rail against in teaching good play writing. BUT. That's for people who are trying to write traditional, mainstream plays that will stage in a proscenium arch and seek the approbation of the largely middle class aspirational theatre goer. (Usually these are the kind of people I've taught playwriting to actually!) And BBBB was not trying to do that.

I saw *The Resistible Rise* at the National in 1991 and it changed my life. Prior to that performance I would have hung Brecht out to dry, being a committed fourth wall realist Stanislavskian trained actor. I went on sufferance, taking an A Level drama group of students to see it. It had Antony Sher as Arturo Ui (and a cast of some 27!) and while it had an immediate impact, it also had a slow-drip feed effect into my own writing which I wasn't to come to acknowledge till probably some ten years later.

The character of Benito Boccanegra is a created fiction. Literally. In the play, Joe Green and his student colleague are writing things up on the board trying to work out an equation for fame based on the letters in a name and as various names get wiped off, the name Benito Boccanegra emerges – and so the character 'comes into

119

being.' (Obviously Mussolini and Simone are the rubbed out bits of name!) Benito Boccanegra then takes the play by the horns, completely unaware that he is just a 'character' in a play. With devastating effects. The underlying politics of the play compares fourteenth century Italy, with nineteenth century Europe and the rise of Fascism in the twentieth century. And the philosophy of the play deals with how fiction and fact are created. This is a theme I've come back to time and again in my plays – getting ever more 'out there' it seems. Throw in my reading of *Six Characters in Search of an Author* and the beginning of my desire to play with theatrical boxes really started to grow.

Obviously the world of the theatre is a fictionally created world. There is a relationship between characters, actors and audience which I find fascinating. Creating reality works on so many levels both in life and in drama. The relationship between what you see and what's happening underneath and what reality can possibly mean in drama is core to my work and my interest in all aspects of the drama.

Perhaps it's not surprising that, over the years, I developed a strange quantum version of realism and absurdism in my work. Perhaps it was inevitable. Perhaps it's my own, unique contribution to the history of theatre, if that's not too pretentious. It's certainly kept my mind active over twenty years and maybe that's enough. Audiences have their own rules. Communicating with an audience is a transient and flexible thing and it's very difficult to assess how well or badly one achieves this symbiotic relationship, especially in a traditional theatre environment.

To sum up at this stage: for me, as well as being a personal place of sanctuary, the theatre was also a place for politics and philosophy. But I had still to work out the complex relationship between theatre and drama and what my place, and contribution, would be.

MIDDLE

Anniversaries – Bond is Back.

I've learned to be a 'live in the moment' sort of person. Theatre has been important in teaching me that. It used to upset me that theatre was so transitory – a lived experience which lasted the length of the play and (unless you went back time after time to the same production – which believe me, I have done) you cannot get 'the moment' back again. And even if you do revisit the play time after time, the beauty and perhaps the power of live theatre is that every performance is unique. I learned this most substantially during the two week run of *We Wove A Web in Childhood.* Not only do the actors perform slightly differently each time, but the impact of the audience changes things. I never got bored through the whole two week run where I watched the performance and the audience alike from the back of the theatre (apart from the two days I understudied and so was on stage). I learned something new every day. I could have (and still think I could) watch the play day after day live and learn something each time. You can watch a film (or filmed version) time after time and see and learn new things, but there's a fundamental difference. Watching a filmed performance it is YOU who changes with each viewing. With live theatre it is the WHOLE thing that changes with each performance.

So, once you realise that with theatre (as with life) what you get is one crack at the experience (even if you are subject to eternal return) you can settle into it as a creative form and not worry about the fact that every little nuance you've worked so hard on will be lost the moment it passes. The acres of hard work that are not seen, the depth that is missed, or the substance that is either ignored or avoided by an audience (or individual audience members because I'm not a great believer in 'the audience' as an actual entity) are part of it. You put in more than you get out. That's creativity. Except it's not strictly true. As the creator you get out things which never fully get communicated, that's more true. But that's the nature of communication, creative or otherwise. It's a two way street and there are limitations on full understanding between people. In that, I believe, life totally reflects art.

In the mid 1990's I had more or less turned my back on the theatre. Too expensive. Too ephemeral. Too... well, I was a working screenwriter and I spent all my spare time in movie theatres or the BFI library. In those days it wasn't so easy to get hold of a screenplay. And believe me, if you want to write for the screen you not only need to watch films (or TV) you need to read the scripts as well. It's a technical discipline and as with all creative work, an apprenticeship needs to be served.

But in a strange, crossover sort of experience, I wrote *Bond is Back* in the mid 90's. It was an *Abigail's Party* meets *James Bond* type of theatrical experience. The idea might have come to me when I sat behind Mike Leigh at a performance of something (I can't remember what) at the National! I don't know if that's true, but it makes a nice story. Did I imagine the play would ever get made?

Probably not. Although come the 40th anniversary celebrations in 2002 there was quite a flurry of interest with my agent. It nearly got produced. It didn't. It sat around again till I ebook published it in time for the 50th anniversary of the Bond Franchise. I'm resigned to it never being produced. Never be seen by me except in my own head. Which is not the best place to 'see' a play – but it's a lot cheaper and less tiring than trying to get a play put on, believe me.

Bond is Back is funny. It's social drama. It's set at the fortieth birthday party of Kevin (think Timothy Spall) and his childhood friends all get together in a toe cringeingly 'theme' party which rather inevitably goes horribly wrong. How I moved from the Brecht/Stoppard to the Ayckbourn style (because it's more Ayckbourn than Leigh) I just don't know. I guess I was still 'finding' my voice.

The other late 1990's play that never got produced is called *Come Back Molly Maguire*. It was written specifically for an actor friend who had a contact in an Irish theatre in America. It was designed for a traditional theatre environment. It had a cast of four young actors. It had 'correct' length scenes – although Dennis Potter was already lurking around in my subconscious as I'd included a couple of musical interludes – setting some traditional Irish 'rebel' songs to music for the play. I guess it was a play about migration and racism. It was blending the past with the present. A sort of historical drama if you like. But certainly no Ibsen. I don't think it was a bad play. It probably wasn't brilliantly written as I was trying to 'fit' traditional form. I've not looked at it in years. Believe me, for every play I write about in this retrospective there are a heap of unpublished, unproduced works propping up a shelving unit and clogging up a hard drive on a computer somewhere in my house. I can't help it. I work hard at being creative. It's so much better than sales. And so much better than being an actor and having to wait to be allowed to work.

Getting political and getting out and about.

Thus far we've arrived at the mid 1990's and I've had one play produced, retired from an acting career, established a tentative foot in the world of screenwriting, and toyed around with writing plays, not fully understanding that the safety I felt in the plush seats of the proscenium arch mainstream theatre was both an illusion and nothing that would help me in my own writing.

My writing was political. Subversive. Anarchic. Absurdist. I wanted to put philosophy into the theatre if only I knew it. It took me another decade to realise that what I really wanted to do was take drama out of the theatre. That had to wait until I was introduced to Augusto Boal (in writing and later in person.) I see all too clearly now that my 'political' writing was actually an attempt at 'social' drama and it was not the sort of theme that would sit well with the average mainstream theatre going audience.

My mind had become confused between kitchen sink

125

dramas and drawing room farces and political comedies and absurdist drama. Maybe I had over-experienced. Maybe it was time to develop my own way. Maybe it was just time to actually 'do' drama again rather than wait for others to see potential. I was (if only I'd known it) developing a theory which challenges the traditional notion of conflict being central to drama and the necessity for an ordered linear progression in the dramatic arc. But I still thought I wanted to 'play' in the mainstream theatres. I hadn't realised that you can't bite the hand that feeds and get away with it.

I left London behind in 1995, moving home to Scotland. I grew up in the East of Scotland but I moved to the rural South West. Like most people I'd never been to Dumfries and Galloway, only driving past the turn off at Gretna on my way north. But for the next twelve years, and my most productive years dramatically, I lived and worked and created in that region. Despite having the oldest working theatre in Scotland (Dumfries Theatre Royal – where Barrie had his first experience of drama) it's not a theatrically inspired place – Rabbie Burns lived there and I swear you still trip over poets in the fields and towns – and when I wanted *theatre* I had to travel to Edinburgh or Glasgow. In reality this meant the Traverse or the Festival Fringe and RSAMD. I have to say that some of the best productions I've seen are student productions. Actors in training are like Olympic athletes. They are at the peak of their game, before they get fat and bloated sitting around waiting to work and the RSAMD training was (to my mind) an excellent one. I've often used RSAMD students and graduates in my 'fast rehearsal' technique productions and seldom been disappointed in their professionalism or performance.

I had a couple of years of quite serious ill health at this time, and I was earning my living screenwriting, both of which meant I had spare time and gave me the opportunity to experiment with my emerging creative theory. In practical terms it meant I could forget about theatre and focus again on drama. I had to cut according to my cloth and active involvement in theatre had to be in short bursts. But I wanted to use my learned skills in a practical way and so when asked to write a play for young people for a one act play competition, I agreed. I'd not worked with young people for a couple of years but it seemed like a fun thing to do. So I did it.

The result was *The Truth About Hats*. And guess what. It came out Brechtian. It was devised theatre. It was all the things I'd spurned and scorned and denied all those years ago when my idea of theatre was the best seat in the house at the National.

What I mostly remember from the time was the great bunch of kids. We had identical twins and a pair of

127

brothers who were only distinguishable by size – that's a gift for a playwright! I worked with the kids to devise a play about identity and we were all very proud of the result.

They didn't win the competition (let's not go into that one – am dram land again) but one of my proudest moments in the theatre was when the judge (isn't competitive drama a horrible idea?) asked the cast what they thought they were doing in a somewhat shocked tone, because it didn't seem like 'drama' to him. The play had loud music, was pretty in your face and was very much a teenage version of the *Resistible Rise...* where adults are 'hat wearers' who make up ridiculous rules, spreading hypocrisy wherever they go.

The youngest member of the cast pulled himself up to his full height (which wasn't more than four feet) and launched into one of the best explanations of the Brechtian alienation effect I've ever heard. My pride was short lived, half an hour later that wonderful little boy (doubtless a burly man now) was in floods of tears because they didn't win. And he knew they should have done. They should have. It was the best piece of drama on display by a mile that day. I felt guilty that I'd only taught them the lesson I'd learned myself – that if you don't play by the rules you can't expect to win the prizes. For myself that wasn't a problem, but they were in a 'competition' after all. I hope they forgave me. I hope they learned the real lesson which was about the truth of creativity and the strange reality of drama. And that for creativity, the destination is in the journey.

That experience bloodied me a bit as regards youth theatre. It's a responsibility working with young people creatively. I ran several more workshops, all of which were great experiences for the participants and all of which yielded performances which may well have been significant in the lives of the young people themselves. I hope so. But personally, I was learning to move away from the traditional. Moving away from theatre and towards drama. Towards the participation rather than the consumption angle of creativity which marked my latter years where I think I transformed from being a playwright into a dramatist.

Along the way I undertook loads of interesting short projects. I wrote a site specific play *Kirkcudbright's Light* about the artist Jessie M. King. This was effectively a dramatised 'walking tour' round Kirkcudbright and ran (to packed houses?) for some three or four summers.

I taught HNC drama for a year at the local College. The students were great. The facilities were poor and the lighting downright dangerous. I wrote short pieces and directed and generally got down and dirty doing drama. It was great. It's another job I could have continued doing indefinitely had the whole academic/administrative set up

129

been anything beyond woeful. But I wasn't prepared to sell students short and so I gave it away. I lectured at the University and during my residency (more of that to come) I wrote and delivered seminars and live and online courses in stage and screenwriting. I was happy passing on the skills I'd learned.

It's a sort of backstage activity, teaching. And because I love theatre, drama, creativity and writing it never palled to share this with others. I was screenwriting (with increasing unease) for money, but the creative work I undertook in theatrical drama was my life.

Inevitably, I got political. I wrote a short play called *Not Rocket Science* which got workshopped at 7:84 Theatre Company. They so missed the whole political point of it that I don't even want to talk about that any more. Suffice to say that workshop was the moment when I decided I had to 'do' my own theatre/drama my own way. My experiences with 7:84 and indeed with The Traverse (Scotland's new writing theatre) were such that I realised there was something of a major mismatch in our understanding and goals. So much so that I never even bothered to get engaged with Scotland's National Theatre when it became established. The clue is in the word. Establishment. However 'cool' these folk try to be, I'm afraid I still believe that they are working towards a market paradigm which is just not on the same creative planet I'm on. I don't want to play by their rules. So I don't. I choose not to engage with them. There's neither sour grapes nor secret wish to be 'discovered' by them. They don't do what I do. I don't do what they do. End of.

I just finally realised that I would never gain 'acceptance' from this establishment because the very core of what I was doing creatively was against their raison d'etre. It's a shame, it's a sort of deep, picky, philosophical point which I won't go into here (though I can, at length, if requested) but it's just the way it is.

In 2004/5 I had a residency with West Lothian Youth Theatre for nearly a year which again involved workshops and the commission to write a play. At the time of writing the play I had no idea that it would end up being the first play ever performed at the Scottish Parliament, in 2005. Had I known that I would not have titled it *Life's a Pizza.* Imagine. All my life, thinking I was a cutting edge socio-political writer and my claim to fame is *Life's a Pizza.* You have to laugh. It was an interesting project about healthy eating and I think drama lends itself very well to such issue based learning. The play was performed by young actors from WLYT and they ran a workshop after the event.

The central conceit of the play, if such there be, was that a pizza actually contains all the healthy ingredients to make a balanced diet. It's the added FAT which presents the problems. And with more than a passing nod to Brecht again the 'Fat' family who populate the drama tell the story in their own inimitable way. I was beginning to see that there are more slices in the pizza of political theatre than simply the mainstream flavour. Time for Boal to enter the fray. But I'm running ahead of myself. I still have to tell you about the plays that form the backbone of my 'mature' output, before I fully stepped out of the box.

Responding to rural crisis – Men in White Suits 2002

In 2001 I wrote a play because I couldn't not write it. Which is as good a reason for writing a play as I'll ever have. It was a personal response to both the environment around me and the stagnation in my own personal life. It's bleak and deep and the culmination of many years thinking and writing about the lived experience of modern rural life for ordinary people. (Not the ones who keep holiday homes or 'own' large tracts of land.) Foot and Mouth left many people broken and many people just numb. The smell, sounds and fears of that time were palpable and, living on a farm property as I did at that time, I couldn't escape the emotions. It broke communities but in a strange way it also forged communities.

For months I couldn't write anything at all, but then I felt compelled. It was the first time I really wrote 'to bear witness.'

132

Men in White Suits tells the story of a farm in crisis. And a marriage in crisis. Phyllis and Duncan stand to lose it all when Foot and Mouth strikes. The play was given its first rehearsed reading at Lockerbie Town Hall, a year after the Foot and Mouth crisis started. Emotions were still raw and for a rural population it had a realism that would never be matched at the rehearsed reading it was given at the Traverse later that year.

For the Traverse reading the director convinced me to rewrite it, and to take out my rude mechanical urban characters. I was aware then, and am still now, that these characters grate for some people – especially urban people. While it's okay for Shakespeare to write in his rude mechanicals as country bumpkins in *Midsummer Night's Dream,* it appears a crime to subvert that and suggest that urban characters coming to rubberneck in Foot and Mouth regions (as they did) might just get the completely wrong end of the stick. And they did.

However offensive the notion of the rude mechanical urbanite was to a mainstream theatre audience, without this element the play didn't work for anyone, including me. And it certainly suffered in rehearsal from a lack of understanding. While the amateur actors reading at Lockerbie totally 'got' the relationships between the central characters – the sense of hopelessness, isolation and the horrific decisions that people had to make

133

(including shooting a dog) the professional actors (and I suspect the majority of the urban audience) just couldn't understand why Phyllis didn't 'just leave' if her life was so bad and her marriage in tatters.

I suppose people who work nine to five in offices can't be expected to understand how farming life is tied to the land and what that actually means in reality. It's sad that this urbanisation tends to spread out to the acting fraternity as well, though. Getting an authentic rural Scots accent is hard, but getting understanding of rural Scots life was no easier. I'll go out on a limb here and suggest it's an example of the pervasiveness of urbanisation in cultural life within the theatre. People forget that you can't eat a beautiful sunset. Latterly, I've re-read the play and I stand by the rude mechanicals all the way. Sure, they offer something uncomfortable and controversial, but seriously, do you expect a play about foot and mouth to be a happy, clappy experience?

What's interesting to me was that what I was aiming to do in *Men in White Suits* was to present a modern, rural version of a Scottish classic play Ena Lamont Stewart's *Men Should Weep.* I've spent a long time banging the drum for 'gritty rural realism' on screen, stage and print but every time I find myself up against a reality mismatch where the word 'kailyard' is bandied around without any real (in my mind) attempt to understand or acknowledge

134

that Scotland has a very real, rural tradition which is not all green wellies and Landowners but where people live in poverty and work in outdoor factories. Where the home goes with the job and where you marry into a life (don't insult it by calling it a 'lifestyle') which, as Phyllis and Duncan's marriage shows, can be a prison from which you cannot escape.

One day I hope that someone might take *Men in White Suits* off the shelf and dust it down and do some comparative analysis with *Men Should Weep* – perhaps from a sociological perspective. But they'd need to be someone who understands rural life as well as urban life and it's not been my experience to find such a person in the world of 'professional' theatre yet. Until then, like the Foot and Mouth crisis itself, the play will remain forgotten and ignored – that doesn't surprise me at all, even though it saddens me.

Strangely though, the experience of the two readings (rural and urban) did teach me something. It was that however hard I try to compromise, I shouldn't take things out of plays because directors tell me to. While the urban mechanicals might not be to everyone's taste, without them the plays just doesn't work because it loses an element of reality which it cannot afford to lose. It finally taught me that the 'audience' I write for is not the paying audience of the established theatre. And that other people do exist. People who can and should be given the opportunity to experience live theatre which speaks to their lived reality. Not everyone goes to the theatre to 'escape.' Luckily for me, this was around the time I first encountered Boal. It was like coming home.

It was perhaps always inevitable that I would mutate from one style to another. But it was never a given *to me* that I'd forsake Stanislavski for Brecht and then throw them both out the window for Boal.

Let me say right here, I believe good acting is actually very hard to do. To convince someone that what you are doing is 'real' requires great skill and professionalism. Stanislavskian training is (in my opinion) very important in the training of actors. By contrast, Brechtian drama doesn't require the same skills set. No one is being asked to suspend disbelief, even if they are being asked to 'believe' something – and more often than not actually they are being asked to thin about something, or to challenge it. Which means that performing Brechtian (or Boalian) drama well is much easier (for the actor) than performing 'realistic' Stanislavskian drama. As such, it opens the door for many more people to be actively creative.

My personal dramatic journey saw me move from a belief in Stanislavski, through Brecht, to a final acknowledgement of Boal – and that journey took me out of the plush seats and into some very 'real' places. And I don't regret a minute of it.

While on this journey the pendulum has swung between my wanting people to really believe what's happening to the characters in my plays (because it's based on 'real' life experience and, I believe, represents how real people think and act) and wanting people to leave that place of safety (myself included) which is the position of audience in the plush velvet seat, and actually engage with the issues.

At best I think I've manage to somehow meld the two together. I think I've managed to give people convincing 'real' characters who challenge their perceptions of the world whether they are sitting comfortably or not. That's what I've sought to do in the theatre. But theatre isn't drama and I have learned to distinguish between the two.

There is much more to drama than theatre as there is more to my dramatic journey than theatre. And there is much more to my creativity than simply the playscripts. But we're not there yet.

Paying back to Barrie – Down the Line (2002-03)

I had a debt to repay. To J.M.Barrie. In 2002 I started as Dramatist in Residence at Dumfries and Galloway Arts Association, the first Scottish Arts Council Dramatist in residence (funded by the literature department) and the first writer in residence for a while in Dumfries and Galloway who was not a poet. All these points are small but significant in the next stage of the journey.

In the years immediately preceding my residency I could be found often at meetings (I was on the Scottish Writers Guild committee) arguing that playwrights should be paid for writing plays and should not have to 'moonlight' as theatrical producers in order to get their work performed. I believed that strongly. I'm not sure I still do. Actually, it's of no relevance to me any more. I just mention it as one of life's little ironies. Because when I took up my residency at DGAA all was fine and dandy until we came to the point of how we would fund productions. A deathly silence. I don't think the SAC literature department had considered that. They didn't have to 'fund' poetry performances after all. But I pointed out that if I was to enable playwriting within the region it was a reasonable expectation for the emerging playwrights that their work would be produced and performed. And that costs money.

With the old sales mantra 'there are no problems only solutions' in my mind, I took the unilateral step of committing my stipend (the part of my money I would get for 'own work') to setting up a theatre company which would produce work during the residency period. Are you laughing at the irony yet? I'd fought for years not to have to do this and now, here I was, doing it. But it was probably one of the better 'moves' I've made in my life. It opened so many avenues to me, even though I stayed firm to other principles and made sure that I never set up as a 'proper' company which would be eligible for 'proper' funding. That has led to all kinds of confusion from 'the establishment.' How could I be a 'professional' company and not a 'limited' company. How could I be producing work without getting subsidised funding? Ah, *you can't do that* rears its ugly head again. But guess what. You can. I did.

During the six years of Bamboo Grove Theatre Company we put on over two hundred pieces (mostly short plays/sketches). We ran workshops and monthly performances and all manner of outreach, all far away from the mainstream and all of them enhancing the life and experience of local people. It was theatre and drama and much, much more. I engaged with mental health issues, with physical and learning disabilities, with young people, with actors, and with aspiring playwrights and somehow I managed to keep the whole thing afloat. I learned from Grotowski and from Boal and I discovered that small audiences in out of the way places were not a sign of failure. It was the impact you had on the audience that counted. So that's what I aimed for. Loads of people's lives were touched by Bamboo Grove Theatre Company.

139

And I hope in a positive way for most of them.

But back to my debt. It was J.M.Barrie who got me 'into' the theatre in the beginning, remember. Well, in 2002 it was the 100th anniversary of *The Admirable Crichton* and, seeing as I was in Dumfries, in residence, I thought I should do something to mark this. So I wrote an updated version of the play called *Down the Line* and it was performed by HNC students (ably directed by Mona Keeling an RSAMD graduate) at the Minerva Hall, Dumfries Academy (J.M.B's old school) complete with bucket loads of sand for the island scenes, which I don't expect they've ever fully cleared from the cracks in the floor to this day.

The play formed the centrepiece of a Symposium Day at which we also had the eminent Barrie scholar R.D.S. Jack speak. Barrie was given a good outing that day. The play was reprised the following year by a younger group of school children in an outreach project from Oxford University Drama Society. I think my version holds true to the original but yet isn't too 'stuffy' for a modern young audience. *Peter Pan* it ain't, but then Barrie was much more than *Peter Pan*.

Barrie is of course best known for *Peter Pan*, and I 'banged his drum' in Dumfries as hard as I could during my residency. With little effect at the time. But now Joanna Lumley has got behind the Moat Brae Trust and they have got funding for Mote Brae to the tune of several millions. They will set up a centre for children's literature, which is all well and good. I just hope that there's scope for looking at Barrie in a context beyond this one play. Time will tell. Hopefully as a result of all this money spent J.M.B will get more of what he deserves from an audience and readership, not just in Dumfries but across Scotland.

END

Love is an Urban Myth

We are approaching the Third Act or the 'End' section of this retrospective. And it's only fitting that at this point I mention the play which above all others I think represents my 'belief system' both emotionally and structurally.

Love is an Urban Myth was written in 1998 and performed as a rehearsed reading at the Traverse in February 1999 and some months later in the Tron. It was in a way a 'breakthrough' play, though of course it was more like a guerrilla incursion than the stepping stone to any lasting involvement in mainstream (even 'experimental' or 'cutting edge' mainstream theatre) I managed to get the late Tom McGrath to read it and he passed it on to director Nic Bone. I think there was a lot of head scratching but they decided to give it a go, possibly still not sure what to make of it.

When I lived in London for several years a flat opposite had a poster in the window calling out for people to remember the Lebanese hostage John McCarthy and noting how many days he'd been held captive. That stuck in my mind. Later I read Brian Keenan's *'An Evil Cradling'* as well as McCarthy's *'Some Other Rainbow.'* I can recommend both – for different reasons. But both were key to my creation of *Love is an Urban Myth.*   The play is set in a West African prison cell. The 'hostages' are Dave and Sarah. I wanted to explore what would happen if you were stuck in a prison with a person of the opposite sex – someone you'd never met but had been captured together simply because you sat next to each other on a plane. It's a play of relationships. Of the 'games' people play.

And it's a play which has a beginning, a middle and an end. Just not in that order. The first scene is in an art gallery, fifteen years after the 'event' when Dave and Sarah meet up for the first time since the ordeal. This scene pushes the boundaries (and the tolerance) of an audience – it seems meaningless and the conversations are random and disordered. For the audience there's the uncomfortable sense that you are evesdropping on a personal conversation – and you cannot make sense of it because the conversation is intensely personal between the two characters. The scene goes on almost too long to bear. The audience cries out to 'make meaning' and this is deliberate as the intention is to get them to reassess what sitting watching a play actually means. The 'conflict' isn't usual. The audience engagement isn't standard. It's all a bit too... real... too intimate... too absurd. And the audience are in a black box – a sort of prison cell just like Dave and Sarah. And that's where, when the scene ends, we go. Back fifteen years to the prison cell. And now we are all, actor and audience, part of that drama. And everything that happens for the rest of the play allows the audience to go 'oh, I realise what that bit of conversation meant', 'now I get what was going on in the art gallery,' etc.

The structure of the play is built in the first scene and developed in 'real time' through the rest of the play. We are all stuck in the oppression of the prison 'box' trying to work out what love really means. And by the time we get to the final end of the play – back to the art gallery (but even then that's not the end) we, as audience, have been on the journey too. Beyond the end we enter a hotel room – a variation on the intimacy and anonymity of a prison cell – and are really called to consider whether Fitzgerald was right that we are *boats beating against the past'* and whether love is just another 'urban myth' or a game we invent to keep away the isolation of being alive and alone in the world.

My biggest problem, or fear with this play was that Keenan or McCarthy would feel I had trivialised their experience. I mean, I was writing something that was deep and important for me about emotion and human relationships, toying with the notion that 'conflict' in the theatre could be a more intimate and less obvious thing than is usual but I couldn't escape the fact that I was writing drama (even though my own personal experience is riven through the play) and I'd used their 'lives' as part of that creation.

For a writer to use their own life as part of the dramatic narrative is quite acceptable – to use other peoples – I wasn't so sure. I actually met Brian Keenan (at a poetry event) once some years after the play had been first performed, and I spoke to him about it. He was really nice about it and put me at my ease that this was an okay thing to do. I don't do 'heroes' but I have to say Brian Keenan is about the coolest person I've ever met.

He certainly beats a lot of the 'famous' moody types I encountered in London's theatre land years before.

Love is an Urban Myth never really leaves me. During my residency I had the audacious idea to put on three plays in a weekend – calling them a triptych- and it was one of these plays. It stays in my heart for so many reasons. Not least because, to misquote Emily Bronte, to some degree it's true that 'Nelly, I am Sarah.'

The second play in 'Triptych', which was written around 2002 is *When Time Stands Still*. I really don't know what to say about this play. I have mixed feelings. I don't think it's a bad play, I just think that it suffered from being the last play where I tried to ride two horses facing in different directions. It's an homage to the play I loved during my A level English course, *Look Back in Anger* by John Osborne. I decided to try and set a kitchen sink drama on Mars.

The research was amazing. I love to do in depth research because I have this personal belief (probably a throw back to acting days) that in order to understand and 'write' my characters I need to know everything they would know. And since my characters were going to be spacemen on Mars, I needed to know in quite great detail just exactly how you'd terraform that planet. Back in the day, I could probably have been dropped there and known how to build the Hab in which my characters live. It's another prison environment in a way.

What the Triptych plays had in common was mainly that sense of being enclosed in a prison like environment. Looking back with the benefit of a psychology degree to match my earlier moral philosophy one, I can draw some interesting conclusions about the inevitability of my moving out of mainstream theatre into the more flexible and anarchic world of 'drama' because hey, I've written these three plays where the characters (and the audience) are all stuck in a box. The plays are all about the intensity and oppressiveness of the situation and relationships within that situation. And guess what. Perhaps that says something about the writers relationship to her creative form as well! Because after the 'Triptych' plays I burst out of that box bigstyle.

The conceit in *When Time Stands Still* is that time is relative in an interesting way on Mars. Basically there's a forty minute mis-match between the Martian and the Earth day. And for our characters, the way this is resolved to keep them in contact with Earth is that time is 'stopped' (by means of a sedative) for forty minutes each day. But humans being what they are they fight against this. Matti not only stops taking his 'sed' but convinces Elaine to stop too – and they embark on an affair which is bound not to be able to be constrained by this 'unreal' time frame. You need to know that Elaine is married to the other crew member (and Captain) Armstrong. It's a love triangle come kitchen sink drama – set on Mars.

While this play felt fresh and new to me (especially after the claustrophobia of *Men in White Suits)* when writing it, it actually had its origins in the first play I never wrote. I tried to write a play when I was seventeen. It's a little known fact. It formed my 'juvenilia' which believe me

146

was nothing like as impressive as the Brontes. The aim of the play was to look at the Arthurian triangle – from the perspective of Lancelot the night before the final battle. It was called *No Hero I* and I stalled early on when I realised I didn't know enough about love from any perspective to do the theme justice.   But here it came out in *When Time Stands Still*. Matti is a combination of Jimmy Porter and Lancelot. He goes on a bit. Boy does he go on a bit. But that's because that's what (in my experience) these 'charismatic' type seducers do. The world (and in his case Mars) revolve around them. Their life is spend trying to convince others of the vital importance of their own personal reality. Maybe that's why I'm not fully comfortable with the play. Matti worries me. On so many levels. But again, I think it's good for a play to unsettle you. Although I hate those audience 'experiences' where the fourth wall is broken and you are somehow dragged onto the stage and into the action – like they do with you in circuses and pantomimes - I do think that a feeling of emotional discomfort can be a good thing for an audience. But then that's because I don't expect my audiences to be sitting in their plush seats, enjoying their chocolates and somehow distanced from the 'entertainment.'

I want my audiences to feel (to some small degree) the level of naked fear I felt watching Richard Harris 'be' *Henry IV* or Anthony Hopkins in *The Lonely Road* by

Arthur Schnitzer. These plays have long passed into the ether but the emotional memory of them will stay with me forever. That's the power of great theatre and truly great acting. And that's what I aim for in my plays – getting into the head and heart of the individual audience member – making the 'play' real for them in some way. Making them feel something 'real.' I don't *think When Time Stands Still* really does this. Or at least I think the other two parts of 'Triptych' do it much better.

The Other Side of the Mountain

The final play in the Triptych weekend of 2003 was freshly finished with a couple of weeks to spare before the production. But don't let that fool you into thinking it was something I cobbled together quickly to make up a threesome. Far from it. The play originated back in the early 1990's when I tried (and failed) many, many times to find a way to write a play about the last days of Scott of the Antarctic. About those final days in the tent when they lost their hope and lost their minds. Writing madness isn't easy. Writing about real people isn't easy. Realising that they have relatives who might do anything from be disappointed to lynch you is a big disincentive, however honestly you want to write a play.

It took a good ten years of tussling with the concept to change it into something that might work. I changed the setting to rural China. I made the characters 'fictional' and the 'quest' was fictional too.

But it was yet another play about the intensity of the prison. In this case we have Xavier and James who are following a lead across remote Chinese mountains in order to verify the existence of the Daoist philosopher Lao Tzu. Xavier is the scholar and James the mountaineer. They start with fairly fixed positions and views on the nature of life and religion. These change as they are forced to confront 'success' and 'failure' in terms of their discovery and their lives. Like Scott's party, they get stuck in a tent due to bad weather – with the certain knowledge that they will die. And that death takes a long time coming.

Even when I embarked upon writing the play this new way, removing the real people and fictionalising the characters, I struggled with it both emotionally and structurally. Post *Love is an Urban Myth* I was trying to play with structure and for some months I wrestled trying to in some way use the patterns of the i-ching as my structural device. In the end it was too complex but what I did was employ a sort of Eastern structure with the play effectively set into a square rather than the traditional three act linear progressive structure of Western drama. I don't think the audience actually needs to notice this at all, it was just useful for me in plotting out the dramatic journey and character arcs of my work. The basic journey was fairly obvious. From life to death. But I don't believe real life works on a progressive path and I wanted my characters to experience real highs and lows even within the obvious downward spiral. The conflict in the play is really the personal one of coming to terms with the meaning of an individual life. The actual journey is the change which occurs to each character in his world view and in his perception of himself. And perhaps the results are surprising as both characters change when forced to 'step up to the plate' and face the inevitable.

This play expresses some of my deepest emotional and spiritual beliefs and I've directed it (and so seen it performed) with two different casts in 2003 and 2004. Death is never an easy subject to deal with, but *The Other Side of the Mountain* is the best response I've managed to give to that great leveller to date.

Ridiculously (but perhaps inevitably) the space in which these 'box' plays were performed was a beautiful little pros arch/plush seat theatre in Dumfries called The Brigend. I spent a lot of time in this theatre during my residency and while it wasn't the ideal space for the Triptych plays it did offer something interesting in testing my theory that if the play is good enough the audience will not be distracted by the surroundings. I do wonder though, whether playing them in a black box environment might help an audience really experience the intensity of the claustrophobia. But by the time I found the ultimate 'black box' theatre, the Triptych was over, the money and time had been spent and I had to put aside Fitzgerald's eternally backward beating and move on to the next stage – breaking out of the box.

Chasing Waves and Benito Boccanegra revisited

Breaking out of the theatrical 'box' was a long time coming. And yet perhaps always inevitable. From *We Wove a Web* which played in a black box and yet dealt with the melodrama which is so much a part of the history of plush seat theatre, to *Chasing Waves* in which I embarked upon an exploration of 'all the world is in the box', everything I have done in the theatre seems (to me now) to have been part of a whole. I am able to reflect on it because I have left that particular box. Like Xavier and James I'm able to sit back (but in more comfort) and consider what my life in stages has all amounted to. And like James, I'm happy with it.

Chasing Waves was the final play of my residency. It was all about breaking moulds. It kind of encapsulates everything I ever wanted or needed to say about theatre and drama in one not so easy package. Retrospectively I think of it as a quantum *Waiting for Godot*. We have two characters who may or may not be Wittgenstein and Schrodinger, who are not sure whether they are even characters. We are forced to challenge the relationship of actor, character, writer and audience and indeed question what 'the box' itself is. The theatre is a box. The world is a box. Reality is a box. We are all in boxes. And like Schrodingers cat, how can we ever know what state we are in until and unless we are 'observed' by the outside world.

It all sounds very complex - and of course I believe that the way to understand it is to watch it. Failing that to read it. The live 'experience' has only been shared to date by a small number of people who were the audience during the performances at the Swallow Theatre, Whithorn – the black box chosen for the production. *Chasing Waves* was also innovative in that I opened the rehearsal process to 'audience' so that aspiring writers and interested others could experience the box from the inside as well. The play was directed by Amanda Walker-   I had too much on my plate to run the open rehearsals as well as direct and I wanted to view it from a different perspective. She did a great job, as did the actors, but there's a part of me that wishes I'd done it like *We Wove a Web* and been playwright and director.

Chasing Waves was an ending, and marked the final definitive statement on my journey in stages in the theatre and my dramatic journey as a playwright but of course there are no true endings (except death and there is still more to come. So prepare for one more 'episode' or 'scene' which represents some seven or eight years. Time, as you will see, is relative.

EPILOGUE

So what happens after the end? That's the really interesting question isn't it? I remember being a small child at night wondering and wondering 'what is outside infinity' and determined that if I thought hard enough I'd be able to figure it out. I have grown up to accept that some things are just beyond comprehension, however hard you think, and my creative endeavours have been a large part in this acceptance as much as a large part in my attempt to make meaning of the world I find myself in, and communicate my emotions to other people in the hope that I might find some symbiosis. It happens sometimes. When it does, it's magic. But these are moments and like theatre, they are fleeting.

There's an end. There's a lack of acceptance of that end. There's a realisation and then there's closure. That's the final stage of my journey. Oh, and there's a long diversion into a completely different way of living. And I'm still not sure whether that journey is ended or just shifting to another perspective. That's life.

After *Chasing Waves* I tried to write another play. I even tried to get funding for it (what was I thinking?) But I couldn't do it (I couldn't do either of those things actually) It was another black box extravaganza . I hadn't learned the significant lesson of *Chasing Waves* it seems - once you've opened the box you can't go back in there. It was called *Just a Man* and was an attempt to look at the last night of Che Guevara. I wanted to know what he really, really felt and thought as he lay injured in the schoolhouse in La Paz. But I couldn't do it. Because I knew I could never get into his head and do his thoughts justice. I knew I'd just be writing an 'interpretation.' It wasn't a case of editing his writing, as with *We Wove a Web,* though I tried to do that. It was that the 'moments' I wanted to explore were deeply personal, inside one man's head and all I would ever be able to do was interpret them. And as Marx reminded me frequently 'philosophers have only interpreted the world, the point is to change it.'

When I became a playwright I think I wanted to 'change the world' through my writing. I learned it wasn't possible. I changed myself instead. Now, through drama I think I've changed the lives of some people in the world for better and that is something I'm proud of, but I no longer believe that I (or anyone?) can really change the world through plush seat theatre. Boal taught me that and I thank him for it.

Well, I gave up on the Che Guevara play. Though I'm happy to report that ten years later – I do seem to require a long gestation – I have finally found a way to tell the story. But not on stage.

At this point I was already a couple of years into my 'out of the theatre' dramatic journey – the decade that took place beyond the confines of the stage. And the next play I wrote was really the writing on the wall. It was called *Powerplay*. I finished it this time. It draws parallels between the 'rules' of human relationships - especially marriage, and the rules of ice hockey. In that respect it harks back to *Love is an Urban Myth*. But when I wrote it I realised I really had to stop writing for the theatre because after *Chasing Waves* I had not just broken out of the box, I had broken the box itself.

Powerplay would be best performed on an ice rink. And when in the world is that ever going to happen? It's a play that requires all the fizz and buzz of a sporting event and yet retains that claustrophobic intensity of personal emotion which I'm beginning to see as a hallmark of my writing.

I think *Powerplay* was also my realisation of the end of my time as a conventional playwright. By 2006 I was deep, deep into the world of Boalian drama so I barely noticed that I'd finished one kind of writing for ever. I was now so caught up in the new, flexible scripts I worked on for some seven years with ABC Drama Group – a group I directed and facilitated for and with whom I have had the most profound and delightful experiences of my life.

ABC are not a coda to my life's work, they represent a completely different aspect and through them I wrote (and was funded for writing) an amazing series of dramatic works. I developed a 'flexible' script technique which, took the group from presenting a 5 minute play in 2003 *'King John's Journey'* through a 45 minute comedy version of Hamlet called *'Piglet!'* to a full length musical play *'Aiken Drum's Recycled Musical'* with a large cast, many of whom cannot read or write.

If everything I did on the stage was only a precursor to getting off it and working dramatically with ABC it would not be a minute wasted. I have also employed Boalian techniques, adapted, for mental health projects with some success (at least for the participants). The ABC years are documented in the No Labels Drama Group story *'A Week with No Labels.'*

But this is a retrospective and I suppose the ending is that I no longer actively engage in theatre or drama and have not done for the best part of five years. It's a combination of health and personal circumstances. It may be like a death of sorts, but I hope I'm more like a tree in that while I've faced an ending (several endings) there is a sense of seasonal renewal in another form. I succeeded in 'taking drama out of the theatre' and I have now taken drama out of my life. It was a moment. A series of moments. Many years of many moments and they were nearly all good.

Life includes many endings but also as *Benito Boccanegra* points out, it's important to recognise opportunities. I have tried to take them when presented and make them when not. Mostly though, I believe it's important to live in the moment. My moments in the plush seats and black boxes have now become memories – but what more is there to life than moment and memory?

It seemed appropriate to give a new birth to *'We Wove A Web in Childhood'* during the Bronte Bicentenary, if for no other reason than to allow others the possibilities of making some moments and memories of their own.

Cally Phillips, 2016.

Most plays are available as ebooks, published through HoAmPresst. For purchasing information please visit www.aytonpublishing.co.uk

Plays written by Cally Phillips (with producing company where appropriate)

2011 Choices (ABC Drama)
2010 Meat Your Greens (ABC Drama)
2008 Aiken Drum's Recycled Musical (ABC Drama)
2007 FairPlay Dramas (ABC Drama)
2006 Powerplay
2006 The End of the Age of Oil (ABC Drama)
2005 Life's a Pizza, (WLYT)
2004 Chasing Waves (Bamboo Grove/DGAA)
     Piglet (ABC Drama)
2003 One to One with William Buckland (OUDS)
     The Other Side of the Mountain (Bamboo Grove)
     Down the Line (DGAA 2003, OUDS 2004)
2002 When Time Stands Still (Bamboo Grove, Oxford
     2002, Dumfries 2003)
2001 Men in White Suits (Traverse Reading 2002)
1999 Love is an Urban Myth, (Traverse/Tron Readings
     1999, Bamboo Grove 2003)
1997 Kirkcudbright's Light: Jessie M King (DGAA 1997-
     2001)
1996 The Truth About Hats
1995 Bond is Back
1994 Come Back Molly Maguire
1994 Benito Boccanegra's Big Break
1993 We Wove A Web in Childhood (Running Wolf
     Productions)